ROADDmap®

How to Live From Clarity, In Purpose, With Passion, and Profit

Recognize your authentic self and desires.

Overwrite limiting patterns.

Access and harness your hidden gift.

Deliver your dreams by doing the work.

Dimensional Thinking that elevates your life.

Heddy Touré,
DreamBuilder® Coach

ROADDmap®

How to Live From Clarity, In Purpose, With Passion, and Profit

Heddy Toure

All rights reserved. No part of this publication may be reproduced, distributed, or transmitted in any form or by any means, including photocopying, recording, or other electronic or mechanical methods, without the prior written permission of the publisher, except in the case of brief quotations embodied and certain other noncommercial uses permitted by copyright law. For permission requests, write to the copyright holder, addressed " Attention: Permission to reproduce ROADDmap® How to Live from Clarity, In Purpose, With Passion, And Profit book" at TalktoHeddy@gmail.com.

All brand names and product names used in this book and on its cover are trade names, service marks, trademarks, and registered trademarks of their respective owners. The publisher is certified by Brave Thinking Institute™ as a DreamBuilder® Coach.

Heddy Toure

Copyright © 2023 Heddy Toure

All rights reserved.

ISBN: 979-8-8702-1101-5

DEDICATION

This book is dedicated to:

Everyone who reads or listens and whose life, in any measure, is enriched or enhanced by it.

Everyone who comes to know that they are greatly and irrevocably loved, of supreme worth and significance, and uniquely relevant.

Each one who discovers the ease and joy of living from the higher, inner life and its sublime benefits and blessings.

ACKNOWLEDGMENTS

I am deeply grateful to two matriarchs who have had a great influence and impact on shaping my life. Firstly, Mom, you taught me to live a life *__of__* love, the highest call of human expression. Through your example, I learned to love unconditionally. For that, I am forever grateful. Secondly, Mary, you gave me the second greatest gift – you taught me to live a life *__I__* love. You helped me to recognize my innate identity, understand my creative potential, and embrace my inherent worthiness.

Michael, your luminous and insightful life is a beacon, and your faithful love and support have been sustenance. Thank you for always being, not just a brother, but a faithful friend. Henry, your life-long friendship and encouragement mean the world. Dave, thank you for being my fellow Brave Thinker and cheering me forward. Your friendship is invaluable. Thank you, Kelsey, for your editing assistance, bright spirit, and delightfully engaging presence. My darlings, Summer, Saniyah, Emani, Jaidyn, and Elijah – you're my best and my daily motivation. I love you with all my heart.

TABLE OF CONTENTS

PREFACE 1
INTRODUCTION 9
1 RULES OF THE ROADD 13
2 BEAUTY FOR ASHES, JOY FOR MOURNING 19
3 LEANING INTO THE LEARNING CURVE 27
4 RECOGNIZING YOUR HIDDEN GIFT 33
5 IT'S ALL IN THE NAME 39
6 RECOGNIZING WHAT YOU WANT 43
7 TAPPING YOUR ABUNDANCE 51
8 NOT ANY SUCCESS, GOOD SUCCESS 57
9 HONORING YOUR HEART'S PERCEPTION 63
10 OVERWRITING BAD PROGRAMMING 71
11 WHERE RESULTS COME FROM 77
12 SHIFTING PERCEPTION 83
13 EMPOWERING POSITIVITY 89
14 RECALL YOUR FUTURE NOW 95
15 NOTICING WHO YOU'RE BEING 101
16 TUNING IN TO YOUR ESSENTIAL SELF 111
17 DELIVERING RESULTS 129
18 DIMENSIONAL THINKING 137
FOR FURTHER READING 147
ABOUT THE AUTHOR 151

PREFACE

—◆—

At a time when my life felt empowered, overflowing, and purposeful, my world seemed to crumble around me. The physical health, fitness, and cognitive sharpness that had served me well began to decline suddenly and rapidly. My life had taken a turn down an unfamiliar alley, and I didn't understand the causes for what seemed like an extreme cosmic disruption of all the good I had been experiencing. It would be years before recovery and restoration would begin its slow and unhurried journey. While a return to my former self seemed less than promising, this fact, in actuality, became my greatest gift.

The suddenness and severity of the disruption of the life I knew caused me, eventually, to evaluate my life in ways I hadn't before. I'd looked to a power that now seemed to be standing off and observing the comprehensive and sudden crumbling of a life I'd known. This was new and uncharted territory. I'd looked to the proverbial hills for my help as long as I could remember, but no help, at least not the help I'd been taught to expect and depend on, was coming. At least not in the way I understood.

Tradition taught me to be a lover of God and others. Serving in my local congregations seemed natural. From the time I was a little girl, I'd watched my mother sing and teach with gladness and enthusiasm. Mom had a zeal and joy that was authentic, demonstrative, and high-spirited. I'd always associated it with her commitment to regular participation in the local fellowship. Like her, and for many years, I was dutiful and devout. Always among the first to arrive and last to leave, it preserved my life in ways I hadn't appreciated. I had an intimate and profound knowledge of a greater, surpassing love, and the unraveling of my world could not dislodge it from me. And I held to the belief that there was some unknown purpose a loving Father had in the suffering that had attached itself to me.

Instead of retreating into bitterness, blame, or victimhood, I began to look inward. Disease and weakness replaced my vitality, and certainties I took for granted began to evaporate, but my confidence in being loved and cared for by a higher power never failed. I believed that if I could trust that he cared for my life, surely, I could have enough trust that the same would be true if I breathed my last. That sense of security of soul and detachment from the outcome provided the mental and emotional space I needed to review the seasons of my life and assess the results I had produced with my time, attention, and energy.

Dutiful participation and diligent service helped to mask but not fill the discontent beneath the surface of my pulled-together facade. I filled my time with church busyness, which I enjoyed and was good at. It was much easier to spend my time in a setting that enabled me to avoid and bury broken-heartedness that needed healing and repair. But like all maladies and weaknesses, it would not remain in the background; it came to the fore, finally, to be addressed and remedied.

I'd come to a place where I could no longer broker the conflict between outer prosperity and inner discontent. My health became dire, and despite dedication to my religious tradition and its practices, adherence to its noble maxims, and trust in the eloquently articulated but rarely delivered promises, I entered a valley. Something crucial was missing, and I had become good at dismissing that fact. Ultimately, my willingness to self-examine, learn, change, grow, and improve ultimately led me to discover my truest identity, greatest gifts, and unique purpose.

The theology of my upbringing taught me that it was my duty to 'press on' as a 'good soldier' - and I'd received no countermanding instruction or revelatory insight to the contrary. So, I continued to give my all. Consciously, I considered myself attractive, articulate, personable, and capable. I'd done university, completed advanced certifications, and had lucrative jobs – all great attributes and accomplishments. But they didn't have the power of themselves to heal or elevate my life. Something was preventing me from living the victorious and enriched life I felt stirring inside. There was something wonderful inside, wanting to express itself in ways I hadn't known how to bring forth.

I had general hopes and aspirations but no sense of specific purpose or direction. I had experience with a loving, merciful, benevolent, and caring higher power, and I believed that the empowered and enriched life was mine to experience and enjoy. So, why hadn't I? At the center of my experience was a single, common presence - a realization that pained me but whose complicated truth was necessary to face. It began a process of recognition and acknowledgment and a quest that led to healing, inner renovation, and recovery. I'd seen medical specialists and had surgeries that saved me from physiological impairment and even death. But I'm referring to a healing of the soul. Life had become acutely uncomfortable and brought me to the humbling conclusion that I alone was the constant in all my experiences. There was an elephant in my living room – to coin a phrase my mother used, making life chronically unpleasant and arduous. And I was unwittingly complicit in putting it there.

Before my valley experience, I had never been curious enough to stop and deeply contemplate my life. Days and weeks were filled with work, evenings with the duties of parenting and multiple weekly functions, and sometimes classes and homework. Time for introspection was not only lacking but wasn't really on the radar. Mentally, I was preoccupied with outward activity and doing everything I'd learned was good, proper, and supposedly beneficial, however imperfectly. I'd spent most of my life looking outward for something to accomplish or looking upward for guidance and comfort. Without better information, I assumed that my furious activity would bring me success, prosperity, and eventually peace and fulfillment.

I never considered that my personal unhappiness and professional discontent were resolvable. It was just how the world worked, and as a believer, I rolled with its punches better than some who did not, but not as well as others who did. Finally, when my bodily health deteriorated, and cognitive function declined to a critical degree, I found myself with the head and heart space to ask, despite doing everything I believed was good and right, why my soul felt so empty and incomplete and my once vital body became weak and diseased.

I understood that bad things happen to good people and didn't assume I was entitled to a pass on health challenges. They can happen and be overcome. Unable to fully function, I began genuinely and humbly searching for answers from above and within. I didn't wallow in self-pity but went to the well of knowledge and asked sincerely why I found myself ill and impaired. Why had joy been so fleeting? Why hadn't I found satisfaction in possessions, quality and lasting relationships, gratifying careers, and religious traditions? I wanted answers and solutions at the speed I was used to living, always on the go mentally and physically. Full recovery, restoration, and a return to a sense of health and well-being, which I desperately wanted, came in trickles, and my pressure cooker style of interacting with the world gave way to an imperceptible, slow cooker process.

Surrendering to the longer process, I felt, at times, a sense of futility and began seeking solace from a source I'd known since early childhood. A source that would be a salve for my disconsolation and with which I could commiserate - the hymns and gospel songs from decades past. Depending on the song, it provided a cocoon into which I could retreat or cheer and elevate my disheartened mood for a period. Those songs supplied comfort but could never permanently satisfy the nagging questions within.

I came to terms with the fact that the life I'd been building was on a damaged foundation from my past. And if I were ever to realize the dreams of my heart, my soul had to prosper and would have to undergo renovation. I began to seek whatever I needed to know to remedy my present and build a richer and more fulfilling future. Discontent sufficiently acute and curiosity adequately stirred, I began intently searching the reservoir of my own soul for answers and solutions.

I'd read about God's promises and listened to sermonic exhortations. Inside the many years of religious tradition, I never saw lives undergo the metamorphosis I'd read and heard of, including my own. I witnessed dutiful men and women waiting for their petitions to show up and their ships to come in age into their advanced years without some evidence that the ship had even been provisioned, let alone left the port.

Promises, articulated in songs and sermons over decades, were long overdue. Confident in the divine love I'd grown to know and experience, I still believed and expected my change, even though I hadn't witnessed anyone else's. Their situations and circumstances remained unchanged despite the many years of routine and devoted adherence. I began to question its efficacy in delivering the life it promised and that I wanted, and felt inside. For me, it was about more than display or appearance. Where was the power to change and transform - the wonder-working power of which we sang and affirmed?

Multiplied years of the same observances and ceremonies had yet to move the needle of my life in substantive ways. The worries and frustrations of the days and weeks continued to greet me in the morning and worry me at night, as they did almost everyone that I knew. I didn't want to remain in the ranks of the walking wounded; I wanted to have a vibrant, victorious life. No longer would I be part of the grand triage; I required more than weekly painkillers and fresh bandages to bolster me.

I needed a salvation that went beyond mental assent, surface appearance, idioms, and rhetoric. It needed to be an everyday, ongoing, living experience I could inwardly sense, see, touch, express, receive, share, and thoroughly enjoy. I was determined to find the real power that would transform not just my own life, but the lives of those I hold dear. It had to be truly exceptional, something that would inspire others to want it for themselves. I needed the salvation that raised me to mastery, not confine me to servanthood. It needed to be accessible, reliable, viable, and lasting.

Introduced to a new idea, I signed up for what I considered a 'clinical trial' of a new treatment that ostensibly guaranteed success without adverse side effects. Filled with hope and eager to be the beneficiary of all its promises, I enrolled in life coaching. That was the beginning of the clearing of ruins that limited my life. Now, someone appeared who understood my condition and could help me turn it around. It was a pivotal moment in my life that began a new journey - one in which I would find the missing pieces, connect the dots, and extricate the root causes of my discontent. It would be a journey of new awareness, understanding, tools, strategies, and support. It promised to help me build an authentic, rich, and deeply gratifying life. One overflowing with intangible and tangible prosperity. Abundant in ways that felt good and could impact the lives of those around me - the thing I most wanted to embody and express.

I was offered the privilege of studying under a world-renowned transformational leader, international speaker, and best selling author. As a global consultant, she worked with Nelson Mandela, the first President of South Africa, the family of Dr. Martin Luther King Jr., His Holiness the Dalai Lama, and spoke at the United Nations. With access to a higher domain of awareness, I continue to learn and apply the principles and wisdom that allow me to develop empowering mental and emotional skills, adopt positive attitudes and make life-enhancing choices. The ability to operate in this higher domain was always present; I simply did not recognize it, understand its rules of engagement, or ally myself with it. I conceded, finally, that the practices and observances to which I adhered would not by themselves deliver its promises or me from the discontent that haunted my life. I discovered that I have the power, ability, and responsibility to live in the potential I felt inside and have the full, abundant, and enthralling experiences that I could only glimpse. As a consequence, I unwittingly relinquished my right to experience it.

I've described challenges that many experience in their personal circumstances. You, too, have a journey into personal purpose and rich fulfillment that is uniquely yours. Some will hear and accept the soft inner call to come up higher, and it will require sufficient curiosity and desire from those who respond. Because you're listening or reading right now, I know you want a pivotal shift in some area of your life, and you deserve it. You're on the right track, and if you persist, you will step into your greatness and live an increasingly full and abundant life that you love.

We are more powerful than we know. Your commitment to this original idea is the beginning of transforming the circumstances and conditions of your experience and living the life you love.

INTRODUCTION

ROADDmap is a simple-to-understand and easy-to-assimilate formula that can immediately improve your experience at any moment; and that you can access and apply to produce new, longer-term results. You are here, not for your life alone but also for those you impact. The ROADDmap framework helps you acquire the mindset necessary to enjoy the life you would love, feel personally fulfilled, and offer your unique gifts and abilities in service to others.

ROADDmap's 5-step proprietary method is easy to learn and adopt. Reach for it mentally and regularly and apply it unceasingly. Prepare to discover your hidden gift and deliver your genius. As you launch into an expanded awareness, you will gain the tools to identify, define, achieve, experience, and enjoy your heart's desire.

Learning the ROADDmap method is simple; applying it will be fun, challenging, and worth your dedication and discipline. Having what you truly want asks that of you. It will require no external equipment or personnel. You'll need no gym equipment or devices to help form and strengthen the muscles supporting your transformation. Instead, you'll access the most powerful and accurate technology without a smartphone or computer.

Think of ROADDmap as your mental rehabilitation and soul-reconditioning program. Use it as therapy, providing constructive counsel and intuitive guidance, and as your assistive device – always at hand to give needed support. You can rely on its age-old wisdom, universal laws, and the experience of men and women recorded over centuries who have engaged its principles. You can also rely on its structural integrity to help you heal what's broken, strengthen what's weak, and improve or replace what doesn't serve your life.

Take ROADDmap as your prescribed remedy, ingesting its concepts and following its recommended dosage: take daily, regularly, liberally, often, and as needed. Appropriate its tools and employ its strategies until, at last, new empowering beliefs and thought processes become your automatic inclinations and responses. Our lives are an expression of our habits formed by years of conditioning. And when we recondition ourselves, we successfully change our automatic reactions and necessarily change our experience.

The idea that we are participants in our own experience is becoming more mainstream thinking. Increasingly, individuals are coming to this awareness and learning how to partner with their world and benefit from its abundance rather than remain a spectator while others savor the sweetness of prosperity. ROADDmap proposes to condense enduring principles and provide a simple, usable mental method so that you can master your circumstances and emancipate yourself from the less than gratifying areas of your life. You don't need to be an engineer or mechanic to understand how to build a car – but it sure is liberating to know how to drive one. ROADDmap method works on the same principle. You don't need specialized expertise to transform your experience and circumstances.

Many would love to experience time freedom, unfettered money flow, greater creative or professional expression, improved health and wellness, and fulfilling relationships. The ROADDmap 5-step mental framework is an actionable tool that integrates easily into everyday life and will remake the person committed to leveling up their experience by diligently applying the learning. The beauty of the ROADDmap framework lies in the fact that though it's universal in its application, it takes you on your unique journey, plumbing the depths of your own authentic identity and desires, unearthing buried genius, and navigating the terrain you will encounter. The level to which you dedicate yourself is up to you. The more frequently and consistently you apply ROADDmap principles, the more quickly and noticeably you will generate results in your daily experience.

As you venture into the beautiful world of your creative potential and begin to practice self-mastery, let me encourage you to be patient, forgiving, and kind toward yourself and others. We are each on a journey and at unique points on our life path. Our job is to be our best selves in each moment and allow others to be theirs – with respective behavioral flaws and challenges. You will soon begin to see that we are part of a whole – that though there are distinctions, there is no separation. And that by being the best you can be, you add to the improvement and uplift of all.

For those ready to step into your potential and live the more extraordinary life you feel inside, this is an invitation and an introductory guide to living in your unique purpose and finding fulfillment, abundance, victory, and the joy of living a life you love!

ROADDmap will:

- Reveal your Hidden Gift.
- Introduce you to your authentic essence and identity.
- Help you determine your unique purpose.
- Uncover your innate superpowers and show you how to use them in service of your dream.
- Increase and expand your awareness.
- Align you with the life you want to experience.
- Build indomitable confidence to pursue your authentic passions.

1

Rules of the ROADD

"In making a living, man has forgotten to live."

Margaret Fuller

If you have experienced chronic discontent in your life in any area, ROADDmap - How to Live from Clarity, In Purpose, With Passion, And Profit will be pivotal for you. In the pages that follow, you will learn the proprietary framework I use to transform areas of my life. You, too, can escape chronic discontent and lack of fulfillment if you're willing to believe it's possible and be disciplined enough to create what you want. ROADDmap introduces you to your hidden gift and the improperly and under-used inherent assets you possess. Recognizing and harnessing them, you'll experience deep personal fulfillment and tap into the flow of prosperity.

ROADDmap's 5-step approach to personal transformation condenses familiar themes from multiple disciplines and puts them into a practical, simple-to-understand and use framework. Experiencing the life you'd love involves developing greater self-awareness, learning enduring life principles and the underlying laws that govern them, and practicing these principles until they become second nature. Changing your outer experience is an interior process, and patterns developed over the years take time to replace. The life you love isn't something you arrive at - it's the way you choose to be every day.

ROADDmap - How to Live from Clarity, In Purpose, With Passion, And Profit may seem to repeat concepts several times. I was, at first, uncomfortable with it. However, I understand that the learning and practice that brings personal transformation and breakthroughs will be repetitive and revolve around a set of inexorable principles. As you read or listen to ROADDmap, be okay with content you feel is repetitive – it's part of your learning and growth process. In fact, I recommend reading this book repeatedly, in parts or completely, to accelerate and deepen your transformation.

Used consistently, this simple framework will empower you to overcome the appearance of every obstacle or setback that confronts you. Because its wealth of principles, insights, and practices are in a compact, innovative methodology, it's easy to remember, and you can access it instantly and immediately shift any area at any moment.

The first five letters in ROADDmap are an acronym for the five pillars in this framework. They are:

Recognizing - Who you are and what you want.

Overwriting - Limiting patterns from the past.

Accessing - And harnessing your hidden gift.

Delivering - Your dreams by taking aligned action.

Dimensional Thinking - By elevating your perspective.

Applying these powerful principles, using the tools, and practicing the skills, you will repeatedly and consistently build, deepen, and consequently self-improve in three areas. The first area you'll notice is improved self-awareness. You'll become keenly aware of your own energy, reactions, and interactions. It's important to pay attention to what you notice, even if it doesn't feel good. Doing so will help you to consciously and objectively recognize, assess, and understand your thoughts, emotions, and attitudes, and how they drive your relationship to the world around you.

The second area you will transform is your reactions to stimuli from the outside world. Increased self-awareness will allow you to transform the parts of your character you want to evolve. Reevaluating prevalent attitudes and revisiting what's most important at your core ensures that your choices are in tune with your inner compass and that your interactions are supportive and authentic to your dream. The third area of growth for you will be in self-discipline – your ability to achieve control and command of your thoughts, emotions, behaviors, and desires by directing your inner resources. You'll no longer need to be cajoled, persuaded, or externally motivated to make positive choices and take consistent actions that improve your life. The simplicity of your decisions will be enough to compel the necessary actions, and you'll create new, beneficial habits.

Your eyes will open to levels of understanding previously obscured and discover that you are the hero or nemesis of your own experience. You'll know that you can remake your life and learn that you have everything you need to do so. But you must use your psychological resources more efficiently and effectively. They are the foundation upon which you build and the scaffolding that supports the amazing life you imagine. And they will inform your aspirations, confirm your hopes, and ignite your passion when judiciously employed. You'll discover that your own inner programming has been the catalyst for your unhappiness and hardships, but don't linger there; doing so will take you further into territory you want to avoid. ROADDmap will guide and keep you along the mental and emotional pathways that lead to results you relish and experiences you welcome. Practicing the principles will keep you engaged in restyling your life.

The ROADDmap methodology will replace and update the old, ruinous subconscious beliefs that have produced the life you want to leave behind. New ones, tailored to the life you love, will be installed and help you recognize the internal and external thieves that would sabotage your dreams. Learning to use your innate intellect and developing self-mastery is critical because your life is determined by the trajectory of your moment-to-moment and day-to-day choices. Increasing self-mastery helps you to stay connected to the life you want and makes the journey exciting, meaningful, fun, and rewarding.

With every road trip, there will be traffic, signs and signals, and rules to follow. You'll encounter other travelers and, occasionally, pull off at rest stops to relax your mind and refresh your focus. You'll see new landscapes and discover new places. Landmarks and bountiful fields of opportunity will encourage you, reaffirming that you're moving in the right direction. There will be detours, roadblocks, construction, changing weather conditions, and challenging terrain as you embark on your ROADDmap journey. You may get turned around, lose your bearings, and need to retrace ground you've gone over before. That's good news because it's an opportunity to retake a vital lesson previously missed. Trust this process, trust your highest self, and trust your journey.

On this ROADD trip, you'll need fuel, maintenance, and some repairs on your long and bendy adventure. Be good to yourself, enjoy your journey, and don't be hurried. Take in every landmark of new insight, inhale the sweet aromas of awareness, and learn your lessons. You are strong, you are beautiful, you are gifted, you have purpose, and you are loved. Begin your journey and create the life you love!

2

Beauty for Ashes, Joy for Mourning

— ◆ —

"I've come that they may have life and have it abundantly."

John 10:10

For anyone who senses something more remarkable for their lives than their past or current experience reveals, there is a path to its manifestation. Every man and woman with the natural capacity to think can experience the life they authentically imagine. In our youth, we quite easily and naturally took on the images, attitudes, and persona of being a ballerina or playing in the prestigious National Football League, for example. I can recall putting on my big sister's laced tulle slip and twirling around the living room, completely absorbed in my fantasy ballet world. These were the beginnings of our innate ability to create and express an assumed identity. Without formal lessons or instruction, children automatically access and engage faculties that let them see, sense, and sample things that do not tangibly exist. They enter and express what they want to experience.

Children have a natural ability to imagine themselves as whoever they want to be. This is because they have not yet been influenced by opposing messages that cause them to doubt their assumptions. They are free to explore and engage their mind, senses, and body without having to alter their thoughts. Such an unfortunate and crippling disservice is a years-long process passed on by well-meaning influencers in their young and blossoming lives. Sometimes, whether by words or example, the bar set for them is far beneath their great potential. They lose touch with the innate abilities that are intended to allow them to soar, and by adulthood, their creative faculties, superior identities, and sense of worth are nearly shut down. Societal convention and cultural norms begin to dictate their choices, and what was once an ocean of free and unfettered creativity becomes a desert. The once fertile soil of their imagination becomes barren, choked by dream-killing weeds.

From childhood, we are conditioned to look outside of ourselves for what is meaningful and acceptable. We seek validation, approval, and acceptance and define our sense of worth from those around us. We learn by watching what others do and listening to what others say and unconsciously accept it as the way things are. Our lives reflect the repetitive ideas and messages we've been exposed to. Too many live unfulfilled, stressed, unhealthful, and out of balance and accept this grind grudgingly.

Well, if it is true that a genuinely fulfilling life doesn't consist of things or possessions, then it's also true, fundamentally, that life is about higher and nobler, intangible qualities. An abundant life is prosperous and contributes to a fully joyful and gratifying experience, intangibly and materially. We can look at society's wealthiest and high-profile personalities and witness, at the same time, the most plagued and troubled men and women. Despite having great material wealth and lavish lifestyles, they're unable to master the situations and circumstances of their lives.

You can, if you believe and are brave, accomplish your aspirations and have the elevated experiences you desire. Why spend your energies on others' dreams while denying your own? Why devote irretrievable hours to someone else's marvelous or miserable life, real or portrayed, and leave your own potential unexpressed? Self-mastery is having the awareness and ability to choose the steps that lead to the life you want and live as that person. Don't be intimidated or dismissive of the idea that you can enjoy a higher quality of existence by developing the discipline to do so. Realizing your dreams requires the devotion of your attention and time. You're devoting it to something anyway, so why not the life you would love living?

No one enjoys facing their imperfection and inadequacy, but self-mastery is not synonymous with perfection, and no one gets things right one hundred percent of the time – we all have behavioral flaws and shortcomings. From a mental effort perspective, it may seem easier to continue as we are though unhappy with our persistent results. But settling for a life that doesn't fulfill is a fallacy. Living in chronic discontent is far more costly than pausing, acknowledging, and getting curious about how one can improve themselves and, thereby, their circumstances. The days, weeks, and years of our lives don't have to be driven by subconscious habits and patterns that produce the very conditions we want to avoid. Doing the inner work is the way to permanently improve outer experience.

The good news is though you may not have been groomed for greatness, you can groom yourself. If you haven't come from a family of high achievers or had the benefit of mentors from youth, you can still achieve at a high level. Becoming sufficiently dissatisfied with the way things are and having a willingness to submit to the discipline of personal growth is all you need to get started. You possess intangible, innate faculties that can deliver success into your life, and learning to use them will pave your path to experiencing it.

Personal growth is some of the most challenging work because it uses psychological muscles, not physical ones. Our mental muscles can become atrophied by constant exposure to ubiquitous and pervasive growth-inhibiting content. They require re-conditioning, strengthening, stretching, and use in ways we rarely engage them. As physical muscles are built by a quality diet, regular exercise, and weight resistance, mental muscle requires quality ideas, attention, focus, and repetitive use. This kind of strength training clarifies one's purpose and builds faith and confidence. While others may struggle in the same environment, those who are disciplined and mentally and emotionally self-possessed are able to experience the same circumstances differently - to live above the fray of external pressure and angst.

Shifting habits hard-wired over decades is not instantaneous. Reversing direction in the middle of a stream whose current has taken you far down a particular life path can seem futile. But if you want something other than what you've experienced, you must believe that you can have something different, despite what you have been conditioned to believe and appearances to the contrary. Self-doubt and the opinions of others may question, discourage, or deny the idea that you can do the thing you authentically desire. But the most influential voice is your own, and the most important message is the one you tell yourself.

I recently read an account of an 85-year-old woman who began her new vocation of life coaching. She'd been exposed to a method of presenting the guiding principles she'd lived by for many years and decided it was still possible to share her life lessons using the new framework that she learned. She talked about the many people who told her it was too late, that she was ridiculous for thinking she could, and that it would never work out for her. But she'd fallen in love with an alternative vision for her life – a dream, and she began to live it. Ultimately, her own voice of truth, her passionate faith, and her purpose in experiencing her dream were the vehicles that transported her vision into her reality. She now enjoys teaching, encouraging, and supporting others, helping them discover and fulfill their dreams, and generating income by offering her knowledge.

You, too, are the right age and ethnicity, have the right history, and are in the right place to begin pursuing your dream. All things are possible to the person who believes. Begin with a mental and emotional pause and take a deep breath or two. Get curious about the things you'd love to experience and do, the places you'd love to go, what you'd love to share, and the person you'd love to be. Open yourself to new awareness and challenge yourself to grow and give expression to what's longing to flow from your life. Your unique light, too long dimmed under a bushel, is meant to shine brightly – it's time to set it on a candlestick and let it illuminate your room and your world.

Make allowances for imperfect performances, but never give up – always speak to yourself with kindness and encouragement. Soul growth is an ongoing process and less of an event, so enjoy your unique journey and offer grace to others. Each of us has an immensely powerful creative faculty of imagination. And with it, we create the experiences we have in our world. Our power to create is part of our intrinsic nature - it's part of our spiritual DNA. And we create every day, by design or default, what we experience in the days, months, and years ahead by our habitual thoughts, assumptions, and actions, however unconscious or unintentional they may be.

Each of us is the artist behind the life we have experienced up until now. But, like the woman who chose a new way of expression at 85 years of age, we can have new ideas and design joy-filled, prosperous, and satisfying lives. Simply put, we can choose what we believe. Jesus Christ said to the man whose daughter had been pronounced dead, "Believe only," though the crowd laughed mockingly and scornfully.

Neither are your dreams dead, just dormant. Your part is believing, despite what others or conditions say, and training yourself to think in ways that reflect the great faith you claim. Mustard seed faith may be tiny, but it's packed with comparatively enormous potential.

You can produce something greater than what you've experienced in your life so far, no matter what point in your earth journey you may be. The necessary components and power to elevate your life reside inside of you. Harnessing them to serve and transform your life is the faith that overcomes and saves you from a life of discontent. You may have made unsuccessful attempts to build a business. Perhaps maintaining lasting and high-value relationships seems complicated. Health and fitness feels unattainable, and you can't see a way of improving your finances without the burdensome time commitment. You may feel stuck in circumstances far below your capability or believe you're prevented from advancing by an unfair or even insidious authority. Although you have felt discouraged or lacked the knowledge of how to put things together in ways that advance and enrich your life, there was something inside that kept saying, "There's more to life - there's more for you than what you're experiencing." And you're correct. There is.

ROADDmap reveals the simple but hidden truths that govern your experience, awakens new and lasting hope for personal uplift, and inspires your commitment to living out your new, unfolding identity. Begin your journey, no matter where you are in your experience or how many years you've been on the planet. Let ROADDmap help you discover and harness your intrinsic capacities and produce results that evoke the words, "I love my life!" You are worthy and able, and you were born for this.

3

Leaning into the Learning Curve

— ◈ —

"Begin with the end in mind."

Stephen Covey

We all want to feel good about ourselves and the life we're living. Knowledge of a higher power and laws that maintain the viewable physical world keeps us mindful of an intelligence superior to our own. It instills civility and respect for others as core values in individuals and communities. As we mature, we recognize, increasingly, that acknowledging higher authority is wise. Those who cooperate with its rules and comply with established order safeguard themselves from corrupting influences and avoid falling away from prudent paths. Just as guardrails along highways and cliffs protect drivers, acknowledgment and adherence to the higher laws of order can prevent individuals from going off life's rails and hurting themselves and others.

The laws and principles that govern how we experience personal success and prosperity can also be learned by any man or woman, regardless of age, ethnicity, background, education, financial position, or experience. From victim to victor, from oppressed to over-comer, from broken to healed, from deficient to abundant, and from feeling insignificant to knowing great relevance and importance – they can achieve incredible transformation. You're already these things; you're just unaware that you are or don't know how to effectively access and harness your potential. You're worthy and entitled, and you possess the attributes that bring success and prosperity. However, you must learn how to create it. It won't come to you by any other legitimate means.

Nothing comes into our space, matter, and time world without first existing as a prevailing thought in the mind. The seat that supports you, the device with which you engage this book, and its contents, originated as thought. Everything begins with thoughts. All the creative faculties are the possession of every man and woman who only needs to bring them to bear in a proper way. Traditional thinking can obscure the simplicity and power of these extraordinary faculties. But by pulling back the curtain and examining them, we discover our ability to create beauty and abundance in new and exciting ways.

Each of our lives is relevant and purposeful. Bringing forth our unique talents and abilities is part of the joy of living. We can and should bring forth our good treasure, not just for ourselves, but for the benefit and enjoyment of others. It's by the measure of our life that we can help someone else, so the most outstanding service we can render is to become our best so that we can offer our best. There is no more important person or role than you being your best in whatever role you assume. You can only be your best by accessing and harnessing the superior faculties that elevate you to your best self. Then, you can present the best, experience the best, and receive the best.

Confronting one's negative traits and unattractive qualities is uncomfortable, but doing so can set one on the road to the introspection, self-discovery, and personal empowerment necessary to grow. The individual with the courage and discipline to examine themselves is the person who can live an exceptional life. Self-correction and self-adjustment, not rationalization or justification, is how the soul develops and the person matures. The one who looks to conditions and circumstances for excuses learns to remain a victim. The one who inquires within for guidance, solutions, and answers learns the keys to living victoriously. They discover their purpose and act with intention and determination, stay connected to their source of strength, and trust their enlightened and inspired self. To have better, you must become better, and that is an intentional, internal process that begins in the mind. It's achieved not by religious activity but by religiously practicing the principles that make us better. Begin inquiring how you may improve personally. Ask what changes are necessary to have new circumstances. Be brave and take the wheel of your destiny. Wisdom, love, goodness, power, and faith will be revealed, supplied, and guide you.

If the idea of self-reliance and personal responsibility, rather than deference to a distant power, causes indignation, that's good news. It can be uncomfortable when firmly held beliefs are challenged. In the interest of growing in grace and knowledge, delay judgment and be willing to learn what you don't yet know and expand your understanding. Keep your antenna tuned to what resonates and receive it. Creating a more purposeful and prosperous life will require you to think more expansively, but it doesn't necessarily mean you must dump everything you've learned and love. Be willing, however, to leave the comfortable shore of familiarity, launch into the depths of increased awareness, and discover your greater potential.

The natural senses are inundated at nearly every waking moment. Distractions and distress coming into our awareness through advertising, entertainment, news, politics, music, social media, gaming, job pressures, health challenges, and role and relationship demands all challenge the transforming work we undertake. As a result, the higher senses that deliver us from the external onslaught lie atrophied and weak through a lack of use. Ultimately, we are the highest authority on what we allow to occupy our thoughts and emotions. By relinquishing that authority and abdicating personal responsibility, we give control of our mental reins to influences outside of ourselves. Until we assume command of our thought life, we alone remain the obstacle to manifesting the very life we say we want.

The universe is for you. Contentment, fulfillment, joy, peace, health, financial flow, vibrant relationships, and all you authentically desire is for you. You only need to understand how to access its source, harness the faculties that create it, and be grateful for its abundant supply. ROADDmap gives you the tools and support that anchor you so that you can expect the best and believe in your ability to deliver the dreams of your own heart. Keep growing, learning, and leaning into the life you love. What you desire will move toward you as you continue to move toward it. Overcome fear and remain firm in faith and purpose. Learn from your experiences and extract the good in everything. Strap in for the ride of your unfolding, increasing, wonderful life.

4

Recognizing Your Hidden Gift

— ◆ —

"What lies behind us and what lies before us are tiny matters compared to what lies within us."

Ralph Waldo Emerson

You have the innate ability to live in prosperity and abundance. There are resources and a path to the life you love - you only need to use your hidden gift to access them and discover the path that leads to the life you dream of having. You possess everything you need, but it doesn't happen automatically. I'll reveal your hidden gift and, using ROADDmap's five-step method, show you how to begin having all your needs met, receive the things you want, and experience the life you love.

When you discover and activate your hidden gift, a host of opportunities will appear. Ideas for generating what you want become plentiful, and doing the things you enjoy can become how you earn money. I'm using my hidden gift in writing this book for you. And I use the awareness, mental tools, and techniques that you will learn to transform my experience and live the life I love - so this works when you work it!

As you connect with, think, and act from your hidden gift, you'll experience new levels of inspiration. You'll navigate your world with greater clarity, purpose, ease, and increased confidence and influence. You'll access answers, solutions, guidance, and insights and begin to deliver the blessings and abundance you desire and deserve in every area of your life. You likely have an idea of this gift - soon, you'll understand the power of it and how it works. This hidden gift doesn't need formal training or development; it only needs your attention and discipline to be accessed and harnessed.

Unfortunately, learning to use this hidden gift, which we all have, isn't taught in our universities or primary schools. For the most part, we have to discover it on our own, and we use its abilities in ways that render more unpleasantness than delight into our lives. But I'm so glad you're learning to access your hidden gift, harness its power, and receive the things you want more of. Know this: you must be the engager. Your hidden gift will not usurp your active participation. Nor will it respond to any external stimuli outside of yourself. When you do engage it, you'll discover its potential to deliver what you've longed for and dreamed of.

Have you ever wondered why you haven't gained the success you feel inside? If you're like many, you live in a cycle of disappointment and frustration while looking at the prosperity of others and think it's just for a select and privileged few. NOTHING COULD BE

FARTHER FROM THE TRUTH! Everyone has this hidden gift, but few recognize it. Some tap into it unconsciously and enjoy great benefits and results. Others prefer to do other things rather than what's necessary to access its mastery. But I don't believe that's going to be you. You won't be too mentally distracted or lazy to learn this hidden gift. And you won't allow stubbornness to rob you of its power to change your life and receive what you truly want and deserve. No sir, no ma'am. Not you! You are here, ready to learn, willing to grow, take action, and deliver the abundance that belongs to you. You're what I call a "walker," not just a "talker."

Your hidden gift is the key to all your hopes and aspirations; it has the power, knowledge, and wisdom to bring every idea and plan to fruition. There is no task too challenging, no plan too complex, no circumstance impossible, and no authentic desire unattainable. Your hidden gift is your greatest asset, fierce supporter, and biggest fan. It will never fail you, never lie, and always maintain your highest good as its priority. It's unheralded, but it's reliable, capable, and a faithful ally. You're probably ready for me to pull back the curtain and reveal the hidden gift that's got your back on this level! Well, allow me to introduce you!

You are the hidden gift, my friend!

Let me explain. You are a magnificent being. The Power that's orchestrating, coordinating, and carrying out the voluntary and involuntary functions of your being every second of your life is super intelligent! You are indeed fearfully and wonderfully made! You should pause - right here - and consider this for a moment. Your lungs are expanding and contracting, giving you oxygen and releasing toxins to keep you healthy. Your heart is beating, pumping nutrients to the trillions of cells in your body, keeping you animated every day. Your brain processes everything you see, hear, feel, smell, and taste and organizes it in ways that allow you to interact with people, places, and things for your health, safety, and enjoyment. All of this is so efficient and fast that you rarely even notice it happening. It's an intelligent background operating system that allows you to interface with the world. It takes immeasurable intelligence to perform your intricate bodily functions every day for decades, and it does so without your direct assistance. There is an invisible part of you that is sustaining you.

From your conception, it's been reliable, and it has cared for you. No one walks beside you with medical devices attached to ensure these functions are working - and you haven't done one thing to cause them to - because it's part of you! You have never completed one involuntary bodily function because you decided to - it's happening despite your lack of direct involvement or awareness. Your entire physical life functions without any guidance, direction, request, command, or instruction from you. Your only task is maintaining it by eating, drinking, sleeping, and breathing healthfully. Most people admit to needing to improve in one or more of those areas.

But you possess other intrinsic functions that do require your active, conscious participation and whose attention has gone lacking. Recognizing and using them skillfully, though they have been under-appreciated and misappropriated, will give you the mastery to create what you love by design. You cannot hide or abandon these qualities. You can't leave them in bed when you leave for work or school. You can't even turn them off or put them on pause. They're part of you, sustaining your life, giving you function, whether you pause and consider it with awe and gratitude or neglect to be mindful of its omnipresent care. And when you consciously and felicitously engage them, they will deliver the life you love.

The innate, intelligent power breathing you is more powerful than any situation, circumstance, or condition you may face. Has it not been to this moment? Aren't you still living and breathing? The same intelligence that maintains the systems of galaxies in precise order supports the intricate operation of your immeasurably complex body. It is Intelligent Power. And it expresses itself in you, through you, for you, and as you. By design, you and I want more of the things that enhance our lives. We want more health, peace, fun, convenience, love, time, things to enjoy, places to go, and the list goes on. We're always seeking more of what makes us feel vibrant and happy. It's the source of our authentic aspirations, revealing and expressing its infinite capacity and ability to deliver good things to enjoy in our lives.

And this is your time. As far as we know, we don't get another. Your presence on the planet is limited, and you live in the greatest era we've known. Recognize your identity, discover your purpose, and deliver your gifts now! You cannot act in the past or the future. Now is the time, and today is the day! You possess qualities and abilities meant to serve and enrich your life and bless others. People are waiting and wanting to receive, appreciate, and enjoy the gift only you can bring into the world – the unique beauty and blessings through your singular being on the planet.

5

It's All in the Name

"I am, I exist, I think, therefore I am."

Rene Descartes

You have a wonderful and powerful name. It's the name that reveals your essence and identity. We often use this name in ways that conceal our identity and minimize our potential. Most of us use our original name in a diminishing way, mindlessly, throughout the day. It's one of the things we have to get better at. But from now on, you'll transform that habit by using your name constructively to convey your strength, purpose, and intention. There is virtue and power in your name. Your name is "I am."

YOU are the hidden gift and possess immense faculties of mind. You are a spiritual being with spiritual faculties interacting with the invisible world and realities. Also, you are cloaked in flesh and possess natural senses that interact with the physical world. Notice that I used a lowercase 'a'. You are not omnipotent, omnipresent, or omniscient, but you are a unique stream of intelligent life emanating from it. Inherent divine attributes are also yours - the power to create is your nature, and the license to do so is your right. It's part of your divine design and birthright. It came with you when you entered into the world. You just haven't understood this truth or how to operate in it. I believe that you feel "the urge of moreness" in your being because it's been placed there. Be bold in owning it, learn its nature, honor it, and it will honor you. Your hidden gift is the "I am" that you are!

We've already agreed that, on their own, no one has the ability to breathe, process information, or pump blood through their body. It's done by an intelligence outside our influence and control. This intelligence is commonly called Source, the Infinite, Higher Power, or God. Now, I'm not touting religion or a system of belief here - this book is about helping you perceive the truth of your identity and nature so that you begin to connect with your source of empowerment. You're intelligent because it's intelligent. You are capable and dynamic because it is capable and dynamic. You can design and create a life you love because it designed and created - behold and consider the natural beauty and order in which we live. It is good. Recalling this is essential to creating an abundant and gratifying life with ease, elegance, and grace.

"I am" is who you are, and your role is to use the faculties and capacities possessed by no other species and parlay them into the highest expressions and best virtues of your being. What species can originate new ideas? Which can change their environment? What animal can develop technologies or systems that change how they live and flourish? The things we imagine, whether good and beneficial or destructive, we bring into our world. ROADDmap is a mental tool that assists you in operating from your superior self and bringing out the gifts and beauty inside.

Your hidden gift is your intelligent, unique stream of genius and ability in the world, and it is vested in your prosperity. After all, it brought you into the world and sustains you while you're in it. At some point in your journey, you may have pondered the meaning of life and the purpose of your own presence. Let me offer this as an answer: to express and experience the beauty, wonder, abundance, and goodness YOU create with YOUR life for YOU to enjoy and to share with others. You are unique, and that distinction makes you special. So, recognize who you truly are, reveal your light, and live in your purpose. There is no one like you in all creation, and others are waiting for your gifts and talents to shine forth. Claim these simple, elegant truths and crown your head with this marvelous knowledge until it's anchored in your awareness.

6

Recognizing What You Want

— ◆ —

"The two most important days of your life are the day you were born and the day you find out why."

Mark Twain

Recognizing what you authentically want begins with the seldom-asked question -"What would I love?" As much as we enjoy the things that bring us pleasure, we shy away from asking this of ourselves in a deeper way. Instead, we attempt to meet others' expectations, keep up with trends and traditions, and turn away from our own hearts. Some have had this validating question suppressed for so long it requires repetition and a few moments for the search engine of the mind and heart to return the answer. That you are here is a beautiful expression of love by the power breathing you. All things are for your pleasure as the highest order of being on the planet and of immeasurable worth. Recognizing your identity and worth liberates your mind and frees you to pursue and do what you love.

Getting clear on what you love isn't difficult - in fact, it's really simple to hear from your own heart. The DreamBuilder® Program offers two approaches to answering the question, "What would I love"? The direct approach is simply posing the question and allowing the answers to bubble up. The question may be so foreign that it may require repeating it until, like pumping well water, you begin to generate ideas that feel authentic and energetic. Write them down – this is the beginning of discovering your purpose. When the answers begin to flow, there's an emotional and physical response - tears, laughter, broad smiles, excitement, brighter energy, increased breathing, and the eyes appear to sparkle. You feel the power of being, having, and doing what you love, though not yet actual. And that is the reason you're here - to experience what brings delight to your heart. Consider what makes you light up inside. What makes you smile broadly with delight, lift your hands with deep appreciation, or fold them in profound gratitude? What makes your heart overflow with gladness? What is the highest idea of yourself that you would love to embody?

The alternative approach works in reverse and, for some, may prove an easier route to discover the answers. Consider in what part of your life you feel unhappy or frustrated and where your current experience falls far short of what you would love. That signals that an inner need is unmet or a desire is unfulfilled. It may show up as disappointment, emptiness, anxiety, and other negative energies. Closer inspection and relevant questioning can reveal personal abilities, gifts, character traits, and talents that are under-served and underused by you. Or it could be there are needs within your soul that are going unfulfilled. You may always feel compelled to be involved in something you believe will give you a sense of fulfillment and ignore the symptoms of lingering discontent and emptiness. Busy work only gives the illusion of fulfillment. Inner longing can only be filled by living in harmony with your unique purpose and expressing your true nature.

Whatever the reason you are here may be, it has been beckoning you. It's the call from a deeper, higher self, communicating that it wants to be lived out and felt in your life. No one can offer your gift and talent like you, and no one ever will. Your time is now. Express your unique and lovely light, experience greater fulfillment and happiness, and contribute the good that only you can offer the world. There is something inside of you seeking to emerge. And just as flowers blossom and trees grow from something invisible in the seed, so too are you. Your hidden gift will grow and increase your vision to be displayed so that all may enjoy the fragrance and beauty of your unique expression and contribution.

The seed of your vision requires the good soil of your intention, the watering of your dutiful attention, and the nurturing of your affinity. Cultivate your external environment by exposing yourself to the sun of like-minded and supportive people. De-clutter your life of weeds and debris that choke and subvert your purpose and keep your hands engaged with purposeful action steps. These are non-negotiable dream-building principles, and using ROADDmap will help you focus on them as you develop your creative muscles and deliver the experiences you love.

Recognizing what you want is the beginning of designing the life you love. It's helpful to use a framework in creating your vision by designing it in four distinctive areas. DreamBuilder® breaks down these areas into four quadrants: Health and Wellness, Love and Relationships, Profession or Vocation, and Money Flow/Time Freedom. Improving your experience in these areas heightens your sense of achievement and contribution, increases personal gratification and fulfillment, and positively impacts others around you.

Write out all the wonderful details of your vision. Think in pictures, colors, and movement, and give your emotions to this exercise as you mentally push the play button on your dream life. Remove restrictions from this process. Here, limitations have no place. Be novel and inventive and push the boundaries. It's child-like faith that sees vividly and enjoys vicariously. Your most important task is to remain fully invested in your mental creation. The images and sensations it evokes are the building blocks of your dreams, giving them the energy and structure they need to become reality. Your vision is the blueprint for the things you love - the things that inspire and motivate you from within. Keep it alive by spending time and energy loving and living from it in your imagination and emotions.

Infinite Intelligence has the knowledge, wisdom, and ability to bring your vision into your reality, but you must participate. Maintain your faith, which is substance, and hold firmly your purpose to have them in tangible form. If you waver, return to your written vision and the ROADDmap principles, practices, and skills. There is no failure, only learning and growth. Be an ally and an advocate for your hopes, dreams, and desires, and keep your beliefs, attitudes, and actions aligned with the vision of what you want.

Never feel that you must be locked into any single version of your dream. It's likely that it will require some refinement. Give yourself permission to adjust, shift, change, and redefine your vision. This is your unfoldment, and only you can determine what it looks like and what feels good to you. Do not compare yourself with others. We are each on our distinctive journeys. Some may appear well advanced in theirs; others may appear far behind. It's common for people to offer their opinions, but no one has the omniscience or authority to judge. Refrain from being excessively impressed or disdainful of others. Reserve personal judgment and devote all your mental and emotional energy to the journey that is supremely important, your own.

Expect your vision to evolve. As you move toward its material attainment, you'll gain clarity, and though the essence of your dream will remain the same, it's okay if it takes new forms and directions. Allow yourself the flexibility to receive something different but more extraordinary than you originally planned. The intelligent source of your hidden gift knows all and can surpass the limits of your expectations. It will bring your clear, definite vision and enthusiastic purposes to a happy resolution for you, and all connected to its fulfillment. Keep returning to your written vision, read it aloud, and let it ignite your passion and aim to have what you've imagined. Be excited. Stir your intention. Energize your mind. Take aligned action and generate and maintain your momentum. Never give up.

Recognizing what you love requires that you do three important things. Go to a place perhaps seldom visited - inside to your authentic self, a reservoir ripe for exploration and adventure. Inside your being is a well of wonder waiting to come forth. It's there to discover, demonstrate, and deliver your genius and beauty into your world as only you can. Doubtless, on your journey, some detractive thinking habits and disempowering beliefs will come up for re-patterning. Dismiss or redefine them. Hold onto the good and allow it to blossom.

You'll build the skill of recognizing, acknowledging, and releasing that which would prevent your life from flourishing and return to your vision and intention. Keep discovering and moving along your illuminated path, and always know that more will be revealed in the proper time and manner. The wondrous intelligence seeking greater expression and increase through you will guide you like a beacon to all things for your advancement. If you search, inquire, and follow it, the light of your purpose will shine through obscurity, illuminate your path, and reveal the life destined for you to enjoy and radiate.

Also, you must remain courageous; otherwise, you will be dissuaded and surrender your faith. Doubt and fear are the programming most of us are exposed to. Their nefarious plan to diminish your life shows up in a multitude of ways. In fact, the book of Genesis records it as the initiating idea behind the original fall - the suggestion that caused Adam to doubt his identity, forfeit his status, and all that came with it. No longer should we surrender to fear. We can no longer stay relegated to spectator status, being impressed and awed by the greatness of others and remaining in doubt about our own. Let's come off the sidelines and out of the bleachers and untether ourselves from the falsehood of inadequacy and insufficiency. Get acquainted with your own potential and capacity, and do not trust self-doubt. Set your bar and be faithful to your vision. When you recognize who you are, know what you want, and discipline yourself, nothing and no one can prevent you.

Lastly, be persistent and irrepressible in your belief in yourself and your vision. Endeavor to live from the identity of the person having the life you would love. Be the person you imagine inwardly – it will manifest in your external environment. Always be engaged in the mental, emotional, and physical work of out-living it as you go about your day. Whether it's an interaction in business, with family and friends, or with the stranger that crosses your path, express the essence and virtues of the person you've envisioned and determined you want to be. You are "I am" - the words that come after are yours, and no one else's to fill in.

Jesus told those who desired healing, "According to your faith, be it unto you," and "Your faith has made you whole." Faith is simply the confident certainty and subsequent embodiment of an idea. Your faith will bring into your life what you desire, or the lack of faith will not. Having faith is more than simply believing something can happen. It includes having confidence that you have it though unseen, an undeniable purpose to obtain it, and doing what leads to its actual possession.

We all believe in something - we cannot help but to. It's a built-in, non-negotiable human function. When we learn how to use our innate faculties and believe properly, we live with clarity, in purpose, with passion and achieve our dreams.

7

Tapping Your Abundance

— ◆ —

"The world is full of magical things, waiting patiently for our senses to grow sharper."

W.B. Yeats

Abundance is present, even when it's not apparent. Many see abundance as something out of reach - something others enjoy but not available to themselves. Their lack of awareness and sense of scarcity prevents them from seeing and receiving. But all can benefit from its flow when they recognize its presence, understand its reciprocal nature, and engage with it intelligently. The flow of abundance is for everyone to enjoy, not just a few. And like the natural law of sowing a crop and reaping a harvest, the law of abundance also operates by a cycle of giving and receiving or contribution and compensation. Receiving requires that something of value has been contributed. Farmers give or plant seeds as their contribution to receive a harvest at the season's end. Employees give their time and energy, receiving compensation from regular paychecks for hours worked. Entrepreneurs receive compensation from their customers for services rendered or products provided. Investors receive interest and dividends for the use of their money. You possess talents, gifts, and abilities to contribute, but you must prepare, organize, and bring them to the corresponding market to be exchanged for their value.

You may feel you have nothing to bring for exchange or that what you have has little worth. Again, nothing could be farther from the truth. Your life experiences alone, not to mention your training, education, skills, and work experience, have tremendous value and can help someone avoid pain or accomplish something important and meaningful to them. You only need to develop and offer it. You have all you need, though you don't know all the intricate details of how. When you are aware of and in tune with your hidden gift and tap into the current of your desires, you gain the courage to pursue your authentic passions. You can be a creative contributor and receive value for sharing them with others.

Many have settled for less, not having a clear vision of what they want or feel they have nothing to offer. Limiting beliefs established early often inhibits the imaginative drive and creative abilities. The ability to dream becomes stunted, and the creative wings get clipped. Too often, the case is one arrives in adulthood ill-prepared to thrive and stagnate in jobs that demand one's time and energy but don't satisfy the soul. Frustrated and burnt out, many accept their circumstances as the way life is.

The average worker spends many hours in jobs that they do not enjoy. Usually, this means substituting the development and refinement of one's own natural gifts or talents, sufficiently repressed through conditioning, for a career or vocation of another's design. They acquiesce to tradition, allowing expectations of others and social conventions to dictate their choices. They're trained and encouraged to support someone else's vision, comply with others' demands and expectations, and get compensated for their contribution based on a value others have determined. They do this for a significant portion of their life span, and after they've spent the energies and years of their youth, they get to retire in their twilight years.

There are many for whom this way of contributing brings authentic fulfillment and enjoyment to the soul, and their dedication has helped to increase their families, communities, and the world. Their work has helped more people enjoy more benefits, go more places, and live improved lives, and has brought us to where we are now in our advancement, and we are grateful.

There is, however, a different vantage point from which some participate in the flow of abundance. It's a point of view that discovers and develops the soul, appreciates its uniqueness, understands personal worth, and leverages individuality. This approach taps into inner genius, guidance, and confidence. Tuned to a deeper self-awareness and sense of personal identity and purpose, it trusts and follows innate desire. Joy and gratitude, the mental and emotional disposition that is in harmony with abundance, become the default emotions instead of fear and frustration. And the highest purpose is expressing one's best self, enjoying one's life, and fostering community.

You may think that's too lofty an aspiration. But I want you to consider this question: If someone else can, why can't you? Why *can't* you? Consider the people you admire from afar for their seemingly wantless lifestyle - individuals who have achieved apex levels of success in business, sports, and arts and entertainment. They have the same physical makeup, breathe the same air, and live on the same planet as you and I. You may not aspire to be a C.E.O., a Nobel prize winner, the G.O.A.T. (greatest of all time) in your field, or an Oscar-winning artist. But there is something you would love - to do, have, share or express. Fear often prevents us from pursuing our passions because we hold disempowering beliefs about our ability to accomplish them, our worthiness to have them, or our ability to earn income from them. It's all possible, but you must want it sufficiently and access that part of your being that can achieve it. The rest will follow as you develop new mental skills and soul habits.

The good news is you can discover your purpose, recover your passion, and grow the confidence to elevate and transform your life. You can have a rich and aspiring life because you are the source that contains all you envision and the ability to bring them into your reality. Scientists call this superposition – essentially, the idea that something only comes into being when it receives attention. By creating a vision for yourself and focusing your attention, you generate an energetic picture that, though it is intangible, is real. You've created a possibility.

Taking the reins of your preoccupations, focusing on your vision, and filtering out what is distracting and sometimes destructive, brings you into harmony with what you desire. And you cannot have or experience that with which you are not mentally and emotionally in harmony. The two must agree. There may be decades of a build-up of disempowering, dream-smothering beliefs that have dimmed your hopes for the life you imagined. And while the time for youthful fantasies may have passed, you still have desires; there's still something inside that is longing to be satisfied. You can recover, strengthen, and reinvigorate your dreams or design new ones.

8

Not Any Success, Good Success

*"In the end, it's not the years in your life that count.
It's the life in your years."*

Abraham Lincoln

Part of enduring prosperity is holding unalterable personal standards that align with what you want and that are also universally good. The source from which all things come is unlimited. You may have what you want and need without depriving another of their wants or needs. Waste no energy on resenting what others have or take from anyone what is theirs. Intelligent Power has everyone's interest equally in mind and at heart and will lift the life of all who desire it and are willing to disciple themselves and develop the soul.

The way you operate in the world reflects the things you value. One may value learning and take courses, enroll in lessons, or read voraciously. Another may value relationships and host gatherings or find other ways to connect with people. Some may value being productive and find it difficult to be idle. People who value helping others tend to be avid volunteers and supporters of causes. Take notice of where, what, or with whom you spend the bulk of your time. This is what you prioritize in your life and what you exchange it for. When priorities are not aligned with core values, life is needlessly difficult, frustrating, and void of joy. Whatever you yearn for directly connects to your core values and deeper needs. It's a defining element of who you are, hinting at what you want to express and experience. Your personal values help identify the things that inspire and delight you and guide your choices.

In business, companies establish their core values to define their corporate character - the ethical practices that guide their business conduct. You, too, must have a clearly defined value system that anchors your decisions and actions and keeps you from being distracted by enticements that are extraneous to your purpose. No matter the circumstances, hold yourself to your established standard, even if it appears to cost or cause loss. But be confident that doing so will never cause actual, lasting loss.

Once you have identified and defined your values, they keep the compass of your motive and intention aligned with your vision. The DreamBuilder® Coaching program offers five simple but powerful questions you can ask yourself that, when answered with a firm and resounding yes, indicate that you are in harmony with your authentic desires. These questions lie at the core of what fulfills you.

- Does it make me feel alive?
- Does it align with my core values?

- Does it require me to develop and grow?
- Do I need help from a higher power?
- Does it have good in it for others?

Your dream should be imbued with a sense of excitement and joy and a bit of trepidation. The idea should cause your heart rate to increase and your body to infuse with positive energy. It may bring a smile to your face or laugh out loud. There may be a sense of incredulity or overwhelm at the thought of having it.

It was emotionally moving and humbling when I first allowed myself to entertain a possible version of the life I'd love to live. Even more compelling was the awareness that I had the capacity and power to fulfill it. Looking back, the life I'd lived until then was like a spell, subverting my eyes, occupying my attention, and distracting me from the path of the greater life I felt deep within. Without awareness, tools, and support, I, like most, carried repressed and unhealed pain from my past into my adult life and could not rise above it, try as I might. Subconsciously, my self-image and self-worth were connected to the beliefs that arose from painful experiences in my formative years rather than truth. Someone came along, however, and helped me to understand that my true identity and worth weren't connected to my experiences. I was given a reliable, repeatable method for living from a higher, more powerful identity and experiencing the elevated life I wanted to enjoy. Enlightenment shone on me as never before, and I knew that my life would be expressed and experienced in lovelier, more abundant ways. I'd spent decades listening to well-meaning people and looking in the wrong places for uplift and answers with, at best, temporary results. Now, finally, I heard a clarion call from a heart-centered voice. It taught me to bravely envision the highest dream for myself and to trust that the mind that could think it, my mind, also had the power to create it, and I determined to learn how.

Some may say that thinking highly of oneself is arrogant and not at all humble. Holding a low opinion of oneself is not the same thing as being humble. True humility is recognizing and appreciating one's authentic self, not the self that others cast for you, and recognizing in others the same intrinsic importance and worth. To think authentically of yourself is to know who you are and the incomparable ability that lies within. This self-awareness is a liberating force, transforming and empowering how you think and interact with the world.

You already possess talents, skills, and assets that have gotten you as far as you have. But to have your dream, you must improve, develop, and grow in ways you haven't until now. A dream, by definition, is something desired yet to be achieved. It's something lofty, and to have it, you must be a different person than you have been until now.

If we could obtain our dreams as we are with what we know, we would already have them. We can only advance as far as what we know can take us. The concept was crystallized for me in this way; when we were but small children, we learned that we could get to 25 using twenty-five single digits, or ones. As we advanced in grades and our capacity to understand more complex mathematics expanded, we learned that we could use two fives to get to 25 using multiplication. At even higher grades, we learned that we only needed a single five, and by squaring it, we got 25. In the way more advanced mathematics can be learned, our understanding of the laws that govern life can be expanded. Living our dream can be attained and requires increasing and expanding our awareness. When we do, we see our true selves and see more possibilities for achieving our vision than our current level of awareness will allow.

Since our dreams are intertwined with others, we also require support from people to achieve them. They will be our customers, work associates, partners, vendors or suppliers, spectators, followers, and listeners, and we'll need help from the intelligent universe. You may believe your life is essential only to your family, friends, and maybe your employer. But it's important to people you don't know, those you will never meet, and potentially those that haven't been born. Your gift and purpose are supposed to bring you joy and contentment and be impactful to others in some beneficial way. Depending on your talents and how you express and offer them, you could impact tens of thousands, millions, or just a few. Nevertheless, your unique, individual purpose is part of a greater purpose, and your sense of fulfillment, and to an extent, that of others, depends on you living in your authentic purpose and doing what you came to do. People are waiting to enjoy, learn, receive, and grow because of the gifts and talents you bring to the world.

9

Honoring Your Heart's Perception

— ◆ —

"The heart has reasons, of which reason knows nothing."

Blaise Pascal

More than keeping our physical bodies functioning, our heart and brain are electromagnetic and biochemical relay stations. They produce and emit chemicals and electric pulses that receive and transmit signals that inform our moods, responses, and reactions. One particular function of our brain and physical senses is to signal and alert us throughout our daily journey. When you sense a storm stirring in the air or when you're about to touch something hot, signals and alerts are transmitted so that you consider the course of action you are engaging in more closely. That might mean grabbing an umbrella to avoid getting soaked in the downpour or a potholder to prevent your skin from burning on a hot pan.

As it relates to the life you love living, your intuition and discernment have access to information unknown and undetectable by your physical senses. Part of their function is to give you support to navigate the intangible side of your life safely and beneficially. Signals come through a sometimes sudden and inexplicable knowing or urge. Sometimes they come as strong warnings that are accompanied by physical sensations, such as taste or smell.

I can recall times when alerts, immediate and unmistakable, drew my attention. Sometimes, I heeded, and other times, I disregarded and proceeded with the action or thing I intended. I can say without equivocation that the times I responded and proceeded cautiously or changed my course of action turned out to my advantage. When I did not, I always endured an unwanted and regretful consequence. Some immediate, others over a span of time, all I would rather have avoided. As you navigate your days, making purposeful strides to realize what you want, be open to inner guidance and instruction.

When we're in tune with what we love, we feel a sense of aliveness and gratification. Frustration, tension, and feeling ill-at-ease come whenever we disconnect from our authentic selves. Feelings of pause or uneasiness are a yellow light, cautioning further or deeper consideration before acting. Sometimes, being caught up in getting what we think we want and doing what we have set our minds to do, we disregard the warning signals that alert us. Paying attention to them helps us to make better quality choices, make appropriate adjustments, and take actions that keep us on a harmonious course. I'm not suggesting that you'll make no wrong turns or make no inefficient moves. But they can be significantly minimized when you rely not just on your well-developed plans and strategies but also on your innate senses and inner voice. Highly successful individuals accomplish great things not just because they believe in their vision and have a plan but also because they trust and use intuition to guide the twists and turns of their journey.

No natural person can know everything about a subject or matter. Shift and change are the unchanging fact of our external environment. Science and technology continue to advance humanity by orders of magnitude, particularly with search engines and artificial intelligence. But even that knowledge is limited to historical and current information uploaded onto servers. You, however, are connected to and part of an intelligence that knows all. It knows how to manage and maintain an unimaginably vast system of stars and your physical body's minute and complex systems. Universal Intelligence contains and provides every resource to fulfill your dreams.

A deeper dive into what you truly love helps to clarify what makes you feel vibrant, expansive, and alive. Consider the answers to these questions:

- What things are deeply important to you?
- What are the things you absolutely must have or do to feel fulfilled?
- What are the things that are deal breakers for you?
- What will you not allow yourself to do or be party to?
- What brings delight to your heart, makes you laugh deeply, or excites you?
- What experiences never grow tiresome?

- What generates a sense of wonder?

Questions like these help you drill down to your core values and essential needs.

If it's been a long time since you felt these qualities, recall a time when you did.

- What were you doing?
- Who were you with?
- Where were you?
- What are the qualities inside these experiences that you want to recapture?
- What would you love to do even if you didn't get paid to do it?

See it in your mind's eye. Allow the emotions to bubble up, and enjoy them as you revisit the scenes. This exercise will help you to clarify the things that bring you gratitude, joy, and fulfillment.

Capture the mental pictures and emotions they conjure up with pencil and paper – giving it a visual representation. This is the first phase of your vision's manifestation. The more detail, the better. Be generous in describing what you envision and use verbs and adjectives. Notice the colors and sounds and interactions with others and your environment. Be the actor in the scenes. You may not, in actuality, be living the version of the life you imagine, but you can live it within. Keep it active in your imagination; be the participant, not just the observer. Put it on like the young child in his play and have fun. Emotionalize it - take on the emotions associated with it happening.

Live vicariously. Find smaller ways with what you have, from where you are, to enjoy what will become tangible. If you long for the serenity of living on an oceanfront beach, get some kinetic sand, a miniature sandbox, and a beach umbrella to play in at your desk. If you want the joy laughter brings to your soul, buy a book of funny jokes and keep it handy for a good laugh. If you want the adventure of travel, watch movies or videos about the places you'd love to visit.

Hold and replay the picture of what you desire and, in so doing, cause the molecules that make up your vision to begin to coalesce and solidify in your world. The All - that great universal intelligence and power tuned to every thought, will bring your vision to you as you move toward it. Draw nigh to God, and God will draw nigh to you. Whatever you devote your attention to, you draw near to, and it draws near to you.

Go beneath the surface of tangible objects and mundane experiences to the essence of what those things satisfy in you. Your authentic desires come from within, inspired by the Life that brought you into the world and is breathing you. You can rely on its wisdom and ability to work through and for you to produce and deliver the blessings you want. The Life that's sustaining you is the source of authentic longing and the author of your good aspirations. It's seeking to express and experience through you more of its unlimited potential and abundance. You only have to do your part and work with the Father - the life force from which you emanate and that animates you.

Keep connecting to and pursuing your vision. Have immovable faith and take aligned action. This is where the so-called magic happens. As you do, universal intelligence organizes and orchestrates all things necessary for the material manifestation of your vision and moves it toward you. And since the intelligent universe contains and manages all that is, it can accomplish this reliably, precisely, and beneficially for all. You are never alone or without resources.

You can have and should have things and experiences that delight you. And the man or woman who lives in alignment with the laws that govern abundance and prosperity will have what they desire. But the man or woman who persists in disregarding the knowledge and wisdom that bring about their desires will continue to experience the opposite. They fail to realize that just as the law of gravity will, when adhered to, allow us to fly a 150-ton airplane 30 thousand feet in the sky, and the law of electricity, when correctly followed, enable us to turn on lights in our homes, the law that governs abundance allows us to live in prosperity.

Failing to comply with immutable laws always results in negative feedback in some form. Airplanes fall when they stop complying with the law of aerodynamics. Bulbs don't light up when something required by the law of electricity has gone unmet. So, too, enjoying an abundant, prosperous, and gratifying life requires that we conform to their governing principles.

It's easy to understand that obeying traffic laws keeps us and our fellow drivers safe and makes getting from point A to B orderly and efficient. We know that cooperating with the laws of a free, civilized society allows us to enjoy its liberties and benefits and avoid penalties of various forms. Lasting success and prosperity also work by order and law. Nothing prevents us from having the means, peace, and prosperity we desire except our ignorance of the laws and principles governing them. To live apart from them is to live below personal potential and in antithesis to our own soul.

Discovering your purpose doesn't need to be complicated. You must ask what you would love at the core of who you are. That sounds simplistic, but our default thinking complicates so much of what life intends to be easy. Your path is supposed to be easy to find, clear to follow, and bring you joy. Searching your heart to uncover what it loves will help you identify your inner longings and the avenues and outlets through which you can fulfill them.

When we satisfy our intrinsic spiritual needs and give expression to our purpose, life becomes more fluid and less stressful, more joyful and less frustrating. We notice the beauty and wonder of our existence and lay aside mental toil, fear, and dread. We see the potential of our being and honor the same in others. Being curious about your purpose and listening to the signals and inclinations from within will lead the brave man or woman to new, exciting, and adventurous experiences. The Universe is favorable to you, and the abundance of the world is yours to explore, discover, and experience.

10

Overwriting Bad Programming

"You have power over your mind – not outside events. Realize this, and you will find strength."

Marcus Aurelius

Friend, our experiences are a reflection of the years or decades of input from the world around us. Through impressions from parents and close family, peers, teachers, music, television, social media, and religion, we're filled with ideas that inform our beliefs and attitudes. As developing children, we cannot help but accept their authoritative influence and learn from the words, examples, and models we're exposed to. We define ourselves and the world from their perspective and accept it as the reality of how things are. However, our ideas and thinking patterns are not irrevocably fixed. We can have new outcomes with new information and ideas, clearer understanding, and better thinking habits.

Subconsciously, what we have heard, seen, felt, and experienced makes up the hidden beliefs that we live by. This unconscious programming makes no distinction as to right or wrong, true or false, or good or bad, only what is. The meaning and emotions we attach to our beliefs are the basis for our attitudes and opinions and define the way we interact with others and, generally, the quality of life that we lead. Unchallenged, we continue to think and believe, see the world, and behave and act, or fail to, as we do. We get the same results because we have not yet renewed the contents of our repetitive subconscious thinking.

In adulthood, it can be healthy to re-examine the events and words from past experiences that may have made a disabling impression on our psyche. I emphasize *healthy examination* here. Revisiting the past, as we will discuss later, has the potential to create stagnation and stunt spiritual maturation, which is critical to loving the life you live. But, if you have not yet produced the joy, peace, abundance, and gratification you would love to experience, scrutiny of one's past can illuminate limiting beliefs and be a clarifying exercise. We can change our beliefs and behaviors and produce new results that we welcome and relish instead of living out our days resisting conditions and resenting circumstances. When we monitor and choose the messages that inform us, it empowers us to overwrite the old ones that play out the same unwanted scenarios and enjoy new and exciting results that enrich not only our lives but others.

Understanding how thought patterns form will help you to replace or overwrite the old and nonproductive ones with new, empowering ones that advance your life. Overwriting is a computer term popularized in the 80's. Compact Discs, or CDs, are small plastic disks that store, play, and record digital data. They quickly replaced vinyl records and cassette tapes and spawned the first portable music players. Overwriting describes the process of writing over or replacing existing data on a CD using lasers without the extra step and time to erase the existing data, making them reusable. These CDs were called rewritable, and as long as there was no damage to the disc, they played whatever was transferred onto them.

The human mind is like a rewritable CD. On it has been recorded the lifetime of information and impressions seen, heard, and felt. The healthy infant enters the world able to think, process, and assimilate input and learns to self-express, though it must learn to communicate through language. It's the way we're engineered. When we're born, our minds are a slate upon which those around us begin to write their messages, many overt, much subliminal. We interpret and assimilate their spoken and unspoken messages, and unless they get redefined, the connection that we establish to them remains and impacts our lives, no matter the age we attain. Negative messages cause us to stagnate and live far below our potential.

By nature, we are thinking beings, and it's a powerful, dynamic, creative, and autonomic state. It's happening constantly. Everything we experience in the world has its origin in thought, they are the invisible ingredients that produce all things. If we want something different, we must recondition our thinking habits and patterns with messages that support our desires. We can renew our minds and produce the experiences we prefer by overwriting our current thinking and the beliefs that keep the good we desire at bay.

Most of us would love to experience improved interactions with people in our lives and the world around us. The good news is we can enjoy better personal outcomes, happier relationships, and live more joyfully every day. Our internal conditioning determines our external experience. Our inner world shapes our outer world. To have what you love, you must practice thinking thoughts that will produce it - ideas that align and are in harmony with your desire. Taking charge of habitual thoughts is challenging but rewarding work that requires two vital things: taking responsibility for what we entertain and actively managing our mental and emotional state. We don't get to choose whether or not we will think; our opportunity and challenge is to decide what to think. Thinking is the immutable and unchangeable principle at work within us, and when we use its capacities constructively, it will deliver the good we desire.

Understanding this unchanging principle - isn't it better to hold thoughts that will deliver what you desire rather than allow your thoughts to be dictated to by messages, voices, and images that do not serve you? Do you see why taking charge of what you allow yourself to mentally engage with is critical and necessary if you are going to experience what you love rather than what you want to eliminate from your life?

Knowing how the mind produces your experiences is a great advantage in that it allows you to notice your thoughts so that you are mentally present and in command of them. It helps you monitor what approaches the gate of your mind, decide if it is empowering and positive, and determine its usefulness and fidelity. You can accept, dismiss, replace, or give it a new meaning. Understanding mental processes also empowers you to decide which content to seek out and which to tune out. You can be selective about the content and messages from which your life will unfold, turn up the volume on those that serve your life, and tune out those that do not.

Until we're self-aware, we remain reactive to circumstances and people in our encounters. When someone cuts us off suddenly in traffic or drives too slow in the fast lane, our reaction identifies who we're being in that instance. We can press an inner pause button at that exact moment and shift to a more awakened, conscious state. We can access patience and peace and allow the situation to be what it is without interpreting it in a way that triggers irritation and outbursts.

Knowing that you can choose your response, pause and consider alternative ways of responding, and view what is happening differently. Now, you can recondition your thinking apparatus, see through a new mental lens, and choose an empowered, self-controlled way to be. Think what you want to think, express the higher virtues of your empowered self, and respond accordingly. You can overwrite your current thinking habits and patterns and make your world more beautiful, beneficial, and abundant.

11

Where Results Come From

— ◊ —

"You are here today where your thoughts have brought you; you will be tomorrow where your thoughts take you."

James Allen

Previously, we established that you are a creator. Creating is what you do naturally because it's a built-in function of your being. Every thought, sustained long enough, leads to a sequence of actions that results in the tangible expression of that thought. Our life experience reflects the patterns of thought programmed into our subconscious over time and the habits they've formed. Habits drive our daily lives, and unless we recognize and actively exchange them, it's impossible to overwrite them, and life will continue to unfold in the same ways, with little variation, every day throughout our years. Because they dictate our lives, we must acquire habits and patterns that produce the results we want to have. To this end, this graphic demonstrates how our experiences flow from the initiating ideas from our environment.

Illustration of how our thoughts shape our experiences

I learned about the Results Formula while studying another program. It describes the sequential way we process thoughts and how they integrate into our lives. What we hold in our thoughts and emotions operates in our lives and is expressed in words and actions and experienced in our feelings and outcomes. It's an inescapable principle of our human functionality and happens mostly outside our conscious direction and intention, and often to our disadvantage. Often, we ourselves have been the unconscious culprit in the seeming hardships of our experience. Some who do not claim to believe in superstition actually use superstitious cliches to explain their misfortunes with phrases like I can't win for losing; if it's not one thing, it's another; when it rains, it pours; I guess I'm just unlucky and such like statements. Understanding the Results Formula will help you recognize disempowering messages, choose those that are life-giving and positive, and interpret what you see and hear in a way that serves the good you want to experience and bring into your world.

Everyone has some area that they would like to improve or transform. The good news is that no matter your current situation or where on life's path you may find yourself, you can and should have the experiences you love. Doing so requires you to master your thought life persistently. The Results Formula explains that we attach meaning to the ideas from the external environment. Because our subconscious assumes everything that enters it is true, we form beliefs that support our subconscious assumptions. Strong beliefs engender strong emotions, which influence what we say and, subsequently, what we do. Our experience on the spectrum of pain and pleasure is rooted in internal conditioning.

We've stated that external ideas come primarily from the plethora of people and programming we're exposed to. The 24-hour dissemination of ideas on culture, money, health, fashion, food, relationships, politics and people groups, to list some of the more prevalent themes, inform our view of the world, if unchallenged and unmanaged. The stories we hear become our thinking habits, and we subconsciously accept them as true. We internalize their messages and accept their suggestions, and if the emotional charge is sufficiently strong, we create justifications for why they must be so. When we connect on an emotional level to what we've embraced, even if flawed, inaccurate, misguided, or blatantly false, we speak and act according to them. Just as seeds contain a living force that can produce corresponding fruit, our thoughts are powerful and persuasive and lead to corresponding results.

Unconscious beliefs and associated emotions give rise to sentiment that reinforces them. If you believe, for example, that the supply of money is limited and hard to come by, you feel constricted and fearful, which prevents you from seeing opportunities for increasing your personal supply with ease and enjoyment, and you cannot act on what you do not see. Your attitude and actions will support what you hold as true, and money will not flow freely and easily to you. Your experience will correspond to your belief.

If you believe that no suitable men or women are available to you, you may not appreciate them when they appear; when they do, you won't recognize them because you don't authentically believe they exist for you. If you believe that life is filled with disappointment, misfortune, and struggle, you will not enjoy and value the gift of each moment. Cynicism sees problems and obstacles because the belief affirms it. It seeks and expects negativity and tends to quickly dismiss the positive possibilities.

Actions can only follow the thinking that produces them. Paradigms are the strongholds of the soul or recurring thinking patterns that reinforce themselves. Whether they are empowering and constructive or diminishing and deconstructive, they seek every opportunity and are eager to promote and defend themselves and prove their validity. And they persist until they're recognized and replaced with thinking habits that support the experiences you want to have.

The more frequently an idea is presented for our attention and interest, the more ingrained the thinking pattern becomes. Marketers discovered long ago that it takes hearing a message seven times before it becomes part of our memory, and they use it to condition our thinking and buying habits. They emotionalize their messages with images and music, so the impression is more potent and our responses more automatic. Reactions can range from an inner comment to a mood shift to acting out verbally or physically. Food advertisements are notorious for prompting us to buy their products. I've noticed that I can be easily motivated to make a cup of coffee for no other reason than seeing someone sipping a hot cup of brew on an advertisement or program I'm streaming.

The beliefs you have held over time have produced the results you are experiencing with delight or discontent in any given area right now. But going forward, you can become open to new ideas. You can consider that you're capable of far more than you've experienced - that you have untapped potential and power and capacity to have more for yourself and those you love. The flicker of ideas about what you truly want and how differently you can experience the world is beginning to appear in the scenes of your mind. Possibilities are emerging, and your inherent imaginative ability is bringing them to your receptive mind. Can you feel the gift inside stirring? Are you ready to bring to life what you love and experience greater joy and fulfillment?

Let vision-nurturing and empowering thoughts become your default way of thinking. Begin believing what you formerly considered unlikely or impossible and shift your attitude and outlook. Challenge old beliefs that diminish your potential and dismiss what your natural mind says you can't have or accomplish. All things are possible to the one who believes. Allow a new premise to assert itself as true for your life.

Establish your mind and practice holding thoughts that are complementary to your vision. It's impossible to banish every thought and idea that appears for your consideration. But I'm suggesting that you begin to recognize and deny ideas, images, and messages that are toxic to your vision. I'm inviting you to consider that you're more than a collection of random thoughts or habitual reactions and that you can rise above their limiting influence. Recognize that you can actively and consciously engage your higher faculties, live from your higher potential, and determine your responses to encounters. Show up for yourself in ways that feel authentic and serve your aspirations.

Until now, you've used your magnificent thinking ability randomly, by default, perhaps regretfully, and with unhappy consequences. But you don't have to be an emotional ping pong ball swatted back and forth - letting your mood, decisions, and outlook be affected by things and people around you. You're learning that you can be an informed and skilled architect of your own life - to think what you want to think - feel what you want to feel and respond in alignment with the self-aware and empowered person you choose to be. Be willing to release the thinking that keeps you bound to what you do not desire. Discipline your thoughts, monitor your emotions and words, and intelligently act or refrain from acting. Be mindful about what you entertain, and cultivate a mindset that can receive, grow, and sustain the life you imagine and love.

12

Shifting Perception

— ◇ —

"The only thing standing between you and your goal is the story you keep telling yourself as to why you can't achieve it."

Jordan Belfort

If you authentically envision the life you love, you also feel the energy of having it. Using imagination, you're creating a clear and definite vision and turning unformed potential into unique possibilities. Your dream has form, dimension, color, substance, and vibrancy. It's full of life, love, joy, excitement, gratitude, your gifts, talents, abilities, personality, and character. It's impactful, relevant, and meaningful to others.

Though invisible to your five natural senses, your vision is observable and enjoyable through your higher senses. Overwriting your current conditioning is where you begin to think consciously and deliberately to build and hold new ideas and beliefs around what you want and what serves your life. It will manifest in your world as you practice and maintain the elevated mental and emotional state of possessing it and, regardless of how things appear, take all the steps that bring it into your world.

Of the woman in the sacred text who pressed through the crowds to reach him, Jesus said, "Your faith has made you whole." Hemorrhaging for twelve years, she was unable to experience a whole and satisfying life. She spent years looking to others for help and healing and exhausted her finances with no result. Of the disabled man waiting for 38 years beside a pool of water for another to come to his rescue, he asked, "Do you want to be healed?" The woman with the issue and the lame man dismissed the history of their condition, rejected their years-long stories, and connected with their strong desire. A new, liberating idea and an authoritative declaration challenged the status quo of their thinking, and an electrifying hope emerged. Suddenly alive with hope and possibility, their corresponding actions changed their conditions and elevated their circumstances. They weren't sick or lame in their ability to have what they desired, but they had to shift their ideas and opinions about having what history and appearances said was impossible. For the woman, she needed access to a higher awareness and authority. For the man, he needed his desire and hope re-ignited. Fundamental transformation happens internally first, with a shift of ideas and strong desire, irrespective of how unlikely things appear or how they've been.

Perception is the mental faculty from which this mental skill operates. It's the ability to see beyond appearances or what is known to the natural senses. In dream-building, it's the ability to shift to a new, expanded, more empowering belief. When we attach strong desires and act, things around us begin to form in support of our desires.

The characters from the sacred text demonstrated their willingness to transcend their external conditions and produced the desired results. And you, too, must elevate your thinking to experience what you want. Hearkening back to a previous example, you cannot think there are no good companions and expect one to appear. Even if they do, you can't perceive it because your beliefs only allow you to see what you hold to be true. Your belief and emotional alignment are repellant to welcoming a suitable match.

Suppose you want to grow and advance in your career or vocation, but you believe the deck is stacked against you. That will likely be your experience because your beliefs dictate what you can perceive. And though not every door is an opportunity, you won't recognize those which are, or be reluctant to pursue them. If you believe you have access to a limited amount of money, even though the flow of currency has continued to increase, you may not perceive how you could participate in the flow of multiplied trillions that crisscross the globe. You'll remain sidelined by stories in your own thinking or of others you've adopted, unable to take hold of your birthright of abundance. If you believe your health and fitness are a function of deleterious aging, then you may not be inclined to learn and do the things that keep your body and mind active, alert, fit, and feeling optimal.

Commanding your thoughts and choosing beneficial ways of seeing situations and circumstances keeps you in tune with good. Blessings and beauty are abundant all around us. To experience its flow and enjoy its bounty, match your thinking and emotional energy with the good you desire. Be specific, positive, and purposeful, and hold gratitude. All components of your vision must be coherent, including your thoughts, beliefs, feelings, and actions. Unwittingly, we invite a continuous feed of ideas and information that diminishes our capacity to recognize and experience the good, beauty, and abundance around us. Our natural senses are easily attracted to and distracted by sights and sounds, moving images, and endless trivia. What we entertain, we become familiar with and accepting of. This is why the natural senses alone cannot create nor secure the dreams of your heart. It requires the superior senses - those intangible, spiritual faculties that are infinitely more powerful, stable, reliable, and capable.

Many live in comfort and ease unknown to others. Though this is true, discontent and dissatisfaction pour from the latest news feeds and headlines. Mountains of negative content attempt to force upon our attention, and we have access to it every minute with the tap of a button on our electronic devices.

I don't suggest anyone pretend there aren't unfortunate events and occurrences in the human experience. But the downward pull on our outlook and attitude can be overcome by holding winning ideas. Individual victory is won by committing mental, emotional, and physical effort to every good thing within your power and imagination. Retrain your brain, renew your mind, and guard your heart. You intrinsically possess all that is needed to experience the life you love. It is simply a matter of using your spiritual faculties, gifts, and talents, believing in and guiding yourself, and living from your vision.

Your divine faculties equip you to create, protect, and realize your vision. Guard against corruptive influences by managing mental intake, patrolling thinking and emotional energies, maintaining your vision, and looking for and holding onto the good. It's up to you, and no one else, to use your faculty of perception to keep yourself attuned to the blessings that you want to come to you. Train yourself to utilize your perceptive ability to serve the good you've decided to have and refuse that which opposes it.

Perception can be used defensively and offensively. Defensively, it protects your vision, quenching the appearances and voices that try to oppose your purpose and dilute your faith. Offensively, use it to maintain a winning outlook and attitude about the world. Decide to find the good in everything that comes into your life. Doing so allows everything, both welcomed and unwelcome, to serve and develop you. The presence of good won't always be evident, and there will be times when you must search for it or wait for its unveiling. Insisting upon this principle and maintaining an attitude of gratitude keeps you tuned to positive energy and empowers you to see and receive the blessings intended for you.

13

Empowering Positivity

— ◈ —

"I dwell in possibility."

Emily Dickinson

We see the world, to varying degrees, as either diminishing or advancing. The advancing worldview recognizes the interconnectedness of humanity. It's an optimistic mindset that embraces creativity and believes in possibility. Possibility thinkers move beyond constraints and draw upon their capacity to contribute to improving their condition and, by doing so, that of those around them. The advancing view is a path to progress and success available to the one who chooses it.

The advancing worldview is far less mainstream but infinitely more powerful and advantageous. This perspective emphasizes the importance of self-awareness, self-determination, self-reliance, and controlling where attention flows and which attitudes prevail. This view empowers the individual to participate in their own soul's salvation in an active and informed way, embracing personal responsibility. People who hold this view realize that they have the power to shape their destiny using their superior spiritual faculties. They can break free from external distractions and influences that sabotage their purpose and assume authority in directing their life.

Increasingly, people are discovering that they are the architects of their experience. There is growing awareness that there is infinitely more good and beauty in the world and that the abundance produced on the earth is for the benefit and enjoyment of all, not a privileged few. The person who sees the world as advancing and improving taps into the ubiquitous flow of goodness and abundance simply because their attention and attitude align with that reality. If our attitude is positive, we can find positivity in all our experiences and attract the opportunities, things, and people we are in harmony with. When we actively seek the good and beautiful aspects of life, the same finds us.

The diminishing view sees the world as degenerating and is the prevalent outlook. Heavily influenced by news outlets, entertainment, and social media, this view delivers a continual wave of adverse content that attracts attention and increases viewership. However, there is an overwhelming amount of beauty and good by comparison, and it's a normal experience for many. Still, so many in an advanced and abundant society find it challenging to live happily and contentedly. Human existence depicted in this way creates the notion that life is an unfair, dangerous, and arduous journey that offers scant relief and joy.

It's true that there are ugly and unlovable aspects in our world. But when we adopt this perspective, we accept it as the norm. If we allow ourselves, we become conditioned to view the world as a place of calamity, conflict, injustice, and misfortune. It is not uncommon for people to spend their lives resisting labels, and disproving stereotypes. Which they can never do because it's impossible to change another person's mind, only our own. Living in harmony with who you are and fully developing your gifts and talents, in reality, is the singular, supreme disproof. Living life in resistance to something is exhausting and detrimental to overall health. In part because it means denying one's individual needs and authentic inclinations. Living in conflict with personal beliefs or principles is not only unhealthy; it's a life lived below potential, purpose, and promise.

With constant exposure to a degraded view of society, our optimistic outlook can become cynical. It's almost impossible to find a mental escape. Sometimes we're lost without realizing it. Other times, we don't know how to bring about or sustain the life we truly prefer to live. A lack of familiarity with the inner echoes of our own essential eminence prevents us from pursuing our deepest desires. We often ignore the beckoning invitation of our inner voice because our natural senses are unfamiliar its sound - the dream is too far outside the history of our experience. Simply put, we lack the belief and trust that we possess intelligence, dynamism, and potential beyond our natural ability to detect and direct. So, we avoid risk because we've learned to distrust what can't be verified.

But we can access our superior faculties, learn to use their rich capacities, harness their power, and create the experiences we choose for ourselves. The desire for different, better, more, improvement, and advancement demonstrates the presence of the ability to attain it. Some look to capricious authorities or figuratively cross their fingers and stand aside, allowing fate to deliver its outcome and hoping the result is favorable when it arrives. As creators, we have a built-in ability to accomplish what we desire. We must first turn our focus inward to our personal power and authority and release the captive hold on our natural senses by things or people outside of us.

When you find yourself traveling mental paths that lead to an unhappy state, stop immediately and turn the thought around or change it into a beneficial one. Quickly evaluate distractions by glancing at them and allowing them to fade into the background of your awareness. Begin to unwind the habit of indulging in that which promotes decline, disorder, discontent, and disaster. It promotes the same in your own thinking. Limit the attention you give to information feeds constantly heaped upon the consciousness that discourages, frustrates, and undermines hope. Keep your attention so fixed and focused that you are unmoved and undisturbed by what comes into your mental and emotional line of sight. If it does commandeer your attention, process it and, relying on kind and noble ideas, filter out the good and dispense with anything that hinders your progress.

Just as the vitality of your body reflects the quality of the care it receives, the spirit of your mind will reflect the quality of care given to it. A well-nourished mind thrives on positive thoughts and constructive ideas. Your dream will come by focusing on ideas that develop your talents, gifts, and character; and that support your progress and prosperity. Deny the tendency to spend valuable mental, emotional, and physical energy on that which does not express your purpose or build your vision. Beware of getting caught up in watching others build and advance their lives; get actively involved in creating and advancing your own.

The human mind is impressionable, and it's up to you to retrain it to think on the sublime and maintain an uplifted and encouraged outlook. It's impossible to avoid every negative message, but as the highest authority in your own life, you control one hundred percent of what you entertain and for how long. It is unnecessary to continue living a life that you are dissatisfied with. Matching your outlook and attitude with the good you desire is the renewing of the mind that transforms your experience. You can appreciate what you have and still desire more. But, if you're satisfied to the point of complacency with less than you would love, you don't have to be. Contentedness and complacency are not the same. You can extricate yourself from the latter, and a life of frustration, worry, and stress by accessing and harnessing your intrinsic power and potential.

The triumphant life you feel inside won't happen by simply wishing and hoping. No one will obtain it by complaining about its absence. Proactively and intelligently engage the higher faculties. Assist the movement of your vision toward you by having a firm and unshakable purpose to possess it. Look for internal doors of awareness by exploring your thoughts, beliefs, and emotions, and resolutely participate in your personal change and prosperity.

Seeking guidance and support through prayer is valuable and essential, but you must complement it with proactive efforts toward achieving it. Shift from asking and praying alone into sequential and intentional actions while believing that it's already yours for the having. It will happen when your faith, sufficiently developed, shows up as a commitment to create it with your mind, attract it with a happy and grateful attitude, and receive it through your consistent and aligned actions.

14

Recall Your Future Now

— ◈ —

"Memory is the diary we all carry about with us."

Oscar Wilde

Our memory is a powerful tool, and our capacity for recall is far more useful than we realize. There is another function of memory that can fuel a clear and well-defined vision and expedite its delivery. Just as past experiences can be called up and relived, so can the details and feelings of the future you would love. Because manifesting requires things to develop in our world of space, matter, and time, memory and visualization can be harnessed to confirm the definiteness of your vision and strengthen your faith while it's coming into your real experience.

Future recall rehearses the scenes, sounds, and sensations of the life you've created imaginally in colorful detail. Using memory in this way reinforces your vision and deepens the imprint of it in the subconscious, where habits, choices, and, ultimately, results derive. Visualizing and activating your natural senses in support of your vision strengthens focus and clarity, stimulates inspiration, and drives action. It also prevents your dreams from being thwarted by doubt, distractions, and detractors.

The story of Abraham showcases the power and benefits of visualizing and recalling things that have not yet manifested in reality. A heavenly messenger told him to look at the stars and see their vast number representing his eventual innumerable offspring. His nightly view of the cosmos continually inspired and fueled his belief in the fulfillment of what he held in his mind and heart. Moses was shown the details of the wilderness temple yet to be erected, the details of which he held firmly in his memory. He drew upon the images and emotional experience until the delegated work was assigned and completed in detail, according to all he had seen imaginatively.

These stories reveal the often overlooked attributes and power of our mind's capacity to recall our vision not yet manifest, repeatedly. We have the ability to summon the images and energies of the life we want and fortify our faith until the dream is actualized. When you discover your purpose and define your dream, practice visiting the future version of it. You'll maintain your dream trajectory and imprint the mental and emotional patterns your vision requires before it can become your real-life experience. Future memory embodies the essence of faith – the vision itself is the evidence of what has not yet materialized.

Vision clarity is powerful. A clear blueprint guides your steps and keeps your desire and focus tuned to its realization. What are the pictures you see? What activities are happening? What are the vibrant colors of your vision? Are there fragrant aromas? See the people involved as happy, engaged, and delighted to be part of your journey. Embrace their presence and be grateful for the intersecting of your paths. What emotional qualities do you feel - peace, joy, laughter, closeness, love, generosity, abundance, self-esteem, self-acceptance, confidence, accomplished? Enter the emotional qualities of what you are experiencing. Visualize the conditions that match what you want your life to look and feel like. You are a creator and a creature of habit; rehearse the images and emotions of your vision and adopt the practices that support it.

The faculty of memory has been the genesis of much self-imposed unhappiness. The tendency to call up past hurts or trauma without effective tools and a healthy strategy to overcome their damaging effects inhibits joy and fulfillment in the present moments of life. And present moments turn into years, decades, and a lifetime. It also suspends the development of the necessary spiritual virtues that take life to higher levels of quality and enrichment. I'm sure you can recall recounting a painful event from your life. You can feel the same emotions welling up as if it were happening again. Revisiting, recounting, or ruminating over disappointments and infractions, real or imagined, whether in the recent or distant past, recreates it as though it's happening again. Holding a grudge or having a chip on one's shoulder impedes the flow of greater levels of goodness and deprives the visitor of an increasingly blossoming life.

Many also undermine their own happy future by unconsciously projecting negative images and misfortunes into their destiny through worry and fear. They play an internal, if not verbal, "what-if" game, anticipating unfortunate events and filling their thoughts and emotions with fear or dread. The ill-fated scenarios produced by their own thinking prevent them from experiencing the happy circumstances otherwise available to them.

In the way past events can be recounted and emotionalized, call up the vision of the future you would love to experience. Focusing on your vision in the present with joyful expectations maintains hope and fuels forward momentum. Does anyone begin a journey and drive in the opposite direction? Can anyone drive an automobile successfully while looking in the rear view mirror? Forward progress requires focusing on the present, fully expecting to reach the desired destination.

Forgiveness is a powerful tool for letting go of past hurts and creating an optimistic disposition. Developing and practicing this high-level competency is crucial. Forget past hurts to the extent that it doesn't come easily or frequently into your awareness. Dismiss past offenses to the extent that you no longer mentally rehearse them, emotionalize the pain, or hold others answerable for their perceived misdeeds. Remember that forgiving others doesn't condone their actions but allows the forgiver to move forward without carrying the toxin of pain, anger, and resentment that impede their own progress. While you can't control the deeds or words of another, unburden yourself of unnecessary weight. Develop empowering ways to process negativity as vital life skill.

Welcome new ideas about the life you have imagined and what you can express and experience from a healed, enlarged and enriched heart. Give yourself the liberty of dreaming big. Know that a detoxed heart and creative mind partners with the more extraordinary universal mind to bring you good. By your prevailing thoughts, emotional disposition and prevailing attitude, you can deliver that which you have imagined and ordered. Remember that your thoughts and emotions are things. They're not material, but energetic waves we emit from our being. They are the molecules of potential organizing themselves into the images, events, and activities you have imagined. Let your vision be your contribution of beauty, order, fun, and love in whatever form you bring it forth.

You may not have all the practical know-how or expertise to achieve your vision. No one does. That's part of why a higher, intelligent power is necessary. But just as we don't know fully how a single tiny seed can grow into a mighty oak tree, we don't know how your dream will come into being, but you have every resource necessary for its full expression. Believe that your dream is possible and have faith that it will happen, even though you can't fully comprehend how.

15

Noticing Who You're Being

— ◇ —

"Who looks outside, dreams; who looks inside, awakes."

Carl Jung

We said that your imagination creates and gives definition to your vision. Returning often to your mental picture, using forward memory, and emotionally connecting to your vision keeps you in harmony with the outcomes you want. And your vigilant mental self-management helps you maintain your trajectory. I want to draw attention to another topic of vital and primary importance. A necessary matter for which each individual must assume responsibility - their energetic state.

Feelings are the most transient of human qualities. Given the slightest stimuli, they can change instantaneously and traverse the extremes of the emotional spectrum in a single moment. Erratic and unstable emotions cannot be your default pattern if you want to experience a life you love living. Moodiness and emotional volatility are deconstructive and reinforce patterns that repel rather than attract what you want. Unmanaged, temperamental tendencies lead to complaining, irritability, blaming others, and fault-finding. The reality is moodiness and explosive emotions resist the good you have purposed to obtain, impede its arrival, and cause it to move away from you.

Recognize your energetic state by pausing to notice the signals that manifest. What are common triggers? What thoughts always lead to an unhealthy or unproductive attitude or mood? Notice the shifts in bodily tension like tightened jaws, furrowed brows, or squinting eyes. Are your actions defined or exaggerated by negative emotions? What are the feelings that have taken over the present moment? What beliefs do you have that conjure feelings that are counter-productive to your goals? Monitoring your emotional state will allow you to adjust your reactions during those critical moments on your life path. This self-awareness skill helps you to avoid being provoked by situations, circumstances, or people that could cause you to forfeit the plans for good awaiting you. Does your life reflect the qualities you would love to embody and attract? Before reacting the usual way, pause and notice the emotions behind them and the beliefs that generated them.

The key is to check in with yourself emotionally. Improve your emotional response by shifting your thoughts and beliefs through the power of perception. Notice how you feel, the thoughts and attitudes that arise, and any physical tension present - then choose a more evolved way to dissolve the negative energy and move forward. Beliefs are like crops that grow in the field of the mind and receive their nourishment from their associated emotions. As seeds are to full-grown crops, so are beliefs to our experience. Whatever we think persistently, we come to believe and emotionalize, and it eventually shows up in the field of our lives. A wise woman used to say, "If you don't want an elephant in your living room, don't put it there." Choose to think and believe that which produces the experiences you desire and nurture them with positive energy and feelings of gratitude.

The more you practice emotional awareness, the more automatic it becomes. Soon, it will become the new default mode, influencing your choices, actions, and interactions with others. Your response time will be more immediate, reactions more calm, and results more advantageous. No longer will situations, circumstances, or people impose themselves upon your attention and dictate your emotions. You will determine what messages you will respond to and how. Attempts to commandeer your peace and shake your composure will fail. Your habitual reactions define who you are and are the driving force that defines your day and, ultimately, the sum of your life. Practice the discipline of self-management so that your well-chosen reactions produce happy and welcomed results.

We all want to have more - more income, pleasure, peace, beauty, health, convenience, things to enjoy, and time. The desire for increase is perfectly natural and built into our DNA because the life that breathes and sustains us is unlimited and seeks more experience and greater expression. That's why we have longings, seek adventure, vicariously or actually, and have implacable curiosity. When deprived of the things that increase and enrich our souls, we experience discontent and frustration.

Believing that the desire for increase is selfish or ungracious is a misconception. The truth is that life's aspiration within us is compelling us to express its limitless nature and potential. It is the Infinite working in and through us to experience as much good as we can healthfully handle and enjoy. Our original design included the enjoyment of all good things. The fact that you want more is a testament to that truth rather than a violation of it. There is something beyond your current experience to be, have, do, give, and share. You inherently possess the means to obtain more and can experience more by directing your immense, creative faculties of imagination, intuition, perspective, and memory.

Allow me to summarize the key highlights of the ROADDmap method thus far. Recognize your innate identity, authority, and ability to bring forth the desires of your heart. You possess incredible creative faculties that allow you to experience the world as you would love. Everything begins with and comes to be because of a singular, essential function, thinking. Controlling thoughts, accessing and harnessing creative abilities, and giving yourself direction and instruction are key to having the desired experiences. Managing exposure to ideas is vital because the mind accepts its conditioning, whether it enhances or diminishes one's experience.

The emotional charge attached to an experience determines how impactful it will be in shaping resulting attitudes and actions. It's crucial, then, to challenge the ideas transmitted and received by us and mindfully consider the meanings we assign, opinions we form, and conclusions we draw. The greater the significance and the stronger the emotion attached to them, the greater their power to shape one's attitude and the course of their life. For benefit or detriment, once beliefs are established subconsciously, our lives are governed by them. A person's outer experience always follows their inner experience.

Since the inner world of our thoughts, beliefs, and feelings determines the course our lives take, it's essential to be selective regarding what we allow the receptors of the eyes and ears to be exposed to. They are the conduits to the mind and heart. No one can perfectly control everything that comes into their awareness, but everyone has the authority to give it power by accepting, entertaining, and rehearsing it. We each are the source of our discontent or delight. We prevent or allow our lives to unfold in ways that enlarge and delight us by how we manage the content and movements of our thoughts.

We go about our day on autopilot until something causes us to reconsider our beliefs or question assumptions we've made. If we choose, we can become more curious about our situations and how they can be different and better. Asking quality questions and seeking insight and wisdom will summon the guidance and answers that bring personal transformation. This is a self-awareness practice that proactively sources from the deeper part of our being and connects with our potential and desires within.

It will take more than the current level of awareness to get you to the next level in your experience. Investing in books, courses, people, and programs that expand your awareness and give you tools to build spiritual skills helps you develop at the soul level and increase you. What is unknown, you can learn; what is imperfect, you can improve, and unformed qualities that underpin the level of success you desire can be developed. Building muscles of faith, deliberateness, confidence, perseverance, patience, and determination is a conditioning process over time. All these attributes are essential to experiencing the elevated life you envision, and by consciously employing them, you can create a life of abundance, adventure, and amazement. Life has plans for our good and not distress – of hope and a bright future. We can be amenable and compliant participants and receive from life's inexhaustible flow rather than be led about by the negative bias of the world around us.

A life lived primarily by the natural senses is reactive to events, people, and information around them - what's seen or heard in any given moment evokes a conditioned, habitual response. More than any other time, we have access to an endless supply of news, entertainment, information, and trivia. It takes almost no effort to spend the bulk of the unreplenishable asset of our time being agitated or amused. The ROADDmap method reminds us to respond from a higher level of consciousness - to pause and consider the information in a new light. Before we react or indulge, we can ask ourselves:

- Is it meaningful or impactful to my purpose?
- Does it reflect higher qualities?
- Does it resonate with what I want to express or experience?
- Does it support or detract from the things I value?

- How can I view it in an empowering way?
- What can I learn from it?
- How can it serve the greater good?

Establish, regulate, and maintain your inner environment. Don't be moved by how things appear or what is said. View the circumstances around you in a way that empowers and serves instead of victimizes. The one who regulates their inner environment will self-observe and self-initiate. They have the power to live on a higher plane and on better terms because they are self-aware and manage their inner world proactively.

Such a person is selective of the kind of energies they allow themselves to be exposed to and influenced by, and on balance, choose those which promote the experiences they want to invite. The self-possessed person will not allow situations, circumstances, and conditions or the opinions of others to dictate who they are going to be, how they're going to feel, or what they will do. They take charge of their reactions, call upon their ability to maintain inner peace, and respond with grace and wisdom.

The greater life that you feel inside is genuine and wants to unfold. It always desires to be expressed and experienced. Its unfoldment requires conscious commitment and vigilance because it can be neglected, ignored, stolen, and forfeited. Just as a mother cares for her unborn child, it is up to each one to conceive, cultivate and protect your aspirations and vision. Dreams are born or die in the mind and emotions. With diligent care and attention, you have the power to bring to birth and deliver your wonderful vision, though it may be suppressed for many years.

Tapping into your genius and navigating your exciting new life can be like relearning how to walk. Give yourself the time and liberty metamorphosis requires and detach from needing to know when things will happen or how long it will take. This is a journey of becoming. As with all things, repetition breeds improvement, and you will become highly skilled at accessing, harnessing, and directing your spiritual faculties and creating new results that delight and gratify your soul.

You will stumble and have feelings of discouragement, impatience, and thoughts of doubt as you learn to walk anew. Know that your efforts are not futile; be assured they will produce the thing desired. There is greatness in consistency and persistence. Remember how tenacious toddlers are as their legs get stronger and less shaky, and their steps get more certain until they have firm confidence in their ability. They eventually stride effortlessly, having mastered the skill. You will, too, if you maintain faith, use your creative powers consistently, and stay the course, becoming increasingly the person you want to be and accomplishing the things you want to achieve.

In building the life you love, it's necessary to hold an overriding belief that you have the thing you created imaginally until it becomes a tangible reality. Holding conflicting views about what you want and your ability to achieve it impedes its advancement. Doubt is crafty. When it attempts to slither into your psyche, recognize it and give it no ground. A divided or double mind cannot receive because it is unclear and unfocused. It takes conscious effort, coherent thoughts, focus, and resolve to transform your experience and obtain promises.

Expect to have challenges. What feels like difficulties and disappointments will arise. Remember, they are only feedback, and you can overcome them all. The degree to which you experience setbacks and for how long is determined by you as you choose the perspective and response that serves and supports your vision. Recognize your identity and potential and habitually visit and rehearse your vision. Access your superior faculties and senses, and hold unwavering faith and purpose.

16

Tuning In to Your Essential Self

"We are not human beings having a spiritual experience; we are spiritual beings having a human experience."

Teilhard de Chardin

In a previous chapter, the Results Formula taught us that our feelings derive from the meanings and messages we attach to what we believe. No one has the definitive power to make us believe something or feel a certain way. If we are willing, we can manage our feelings by consciously choosing what to think and believe. Nearly every waking minute, our senses are inundated with an overwhelming amount of information. By necessity, whether we realize it or not, we are constantly receiving messages, assigning meanings, and making choices. Even when we escape briefly, we get pulled back into the cacophony of noise and melee of images and activity. But it serves us greatly when we take time to unplug and connect with the deeper part of our being.

We see Jesus of the bible retreating, often early in the morning, from the crowds, his inner circle, and away from family, friends, and disciples. He spent time alone to connect and commune more intimately with the source of the miracles described in the gospels. He claimed that his Father was always with him and never left him. Jesus wanted others to grasp this essential and elementary truth: that as he relied on the invisible, higher nature that sustained him, so can we; that we are supported and maintained by the same perpetual and limitless life.

Every day, our lives witness Intelligent Power and its transcendency - we cannot sustain ourselves or awaken from our nightly slumber on our own. This Intelligent Power is part of us. Expressing itself through us and as us, we possess remarkable faculties and functions of the mind. Our innate abilities work to bring into our reality whatever we are mentally and emotionally coherent with. Tuning into your essential self helps bring to bear your inherent abilities. Use them to obtain what is yours and live an increasingly prosperous, joy-filled life.

Connecting with your deeper self and using your higher senses is essential to having the elevated experiences you seek. Retreating from incessant external noise and busyness connects you to the reservoir from whence your life springs. Here is where you'll access your intrinsic wealth and, from it, design and deliver the life you imagine and love. Higher qualities of life require operating on higher levels of awareness, i.e., a mental awakening and ascension. Practices that lift you above mundane preoccupations are vital to strengthening the part of your being responsible for limiting you. You want a certain level of prosperity. You can obtain it, but it requires going deeper before going higher. Adopting regular spiritual practices will help you identify your passions, clarify your purpose, and reach your goals. Be open to trying different methods, find what resonates, and allow inspiration and new insights to transform you.

Spiritual practices are essential to staying connected to the empowered, inerrant side of your nature and your vision. Regularly engaging them instills mental discipline and installs the beneficial habits that conduct your dream from potential to real experience. You'll learn to rely increasingly on the invisible, albeit invincible side of yourself and the practices that connect you to it. The after-effect is a flow of gratifying experiences and increased ease and peace along your life journey.

Here are some popular spiritual practices to connect you to your essence and stir your soul's authentic longings. They help you gain clarity and expand your expression and experience of the things you love. I list several and briefly describe some benefits. Add your practices to this list, engage them deliberately, and integrate them liberally into your daily life.

Gratitude: The thankful heart always looks for and expects good. This kind of thankfulness is not a polite response to having received something. That is important and appropriate. However, this is the permanent position of the heart. Being thankful, not for, but in every situation and circumstance, even those unexpected and unwanted. We can generate gratitude by unswervingly holding the knowledge that we are part of a good and benevolent creation despite evidence that would deny it. That the power, wisdom, and understanding that maintains our physical bodies and the vast systems of galaxies always intends our good as its purpose and plan. It's a gratitude generated by willful choice, a permanent attitude of the heart, and is based on inner knowledge and higher truth, independent of appearances or external conditions.

Praise: Just as we rightfully laud individuals who exhibit remarkable actions and achievements, it is even more fitting to glorify the greatness of the Intelligent Power responsible for giving life and sustaining creation. This Intelligent Agent is the source of everything organic and inorganic. It is the originating presence in all and maintains the intricate systems of stars, galaxies, and our world. By incomprehensible intelligence and power, it holds all things together and is the guiding force behind the harmonious workings of the universe. Recognizing and honoring this all-encompassing and incomparable agency shows respect and appreciation for that which is greater than ourselves. It reflects an understanding of the incalculable energy and intelligence that orders the universe and of which we are part.

Worship: Praise is acclaim, worship is reverence. While praise involves acknowledging and acclaiming the greatness of a higher power, worship goes deeper by incorporating a sense of reverence and awe. Worship is a form of profound acknowledgment that transcends mere admiration. As recipients of a higher order of faculties, we use them to express our creativity, solve problems, give and receive love in its many forms, navigate our human experiences, and enjoy the magnificence of our visible world. Worship is the return of profound, deep, and inspired appreciation and adoration for all that gives us wonder and amazement, and from which blessings come.

Prayer: Talking to someone who cannot be seen or heard feels unnatural. Don't let the seeming oddness and awkwardness prevent you. Although invisible, it's generally acknowledged that a higher power works in our personal lives and the world. That it is intelligent and powerful is undeniable - consider the cosmos. Benevolence at work in nature is indisputable; seasons change, rivers continue to flow, trees bear fruit, plants yield sustenance, and the earth produces increase generation after generation. There is nothing closer or more attuned to your every care than the Intelligent life that brought and sustains you. The Intelligence that keeps you is always present, a guide and a helper when relied upon. Ask, seek, and knock. It will bring you the good you desire according to the universal laws, principles, methods, and means it has and will establish. Set aside complaints, worries, and discontent, and trust the transformative energies of gratitude, peace, confidence, abundance, and love.

Devotion: People learn to love and appreciate others within relationships of many kinds. Happy bonds of love are formed by spending time together, listening, honoring one another, and discovering attributes and traits that are endearing and appreciated. In the same way, we can form a greater connection with our own inner qualities and potential. Personal devotion requires consistent time and attention, quiet introspection, self-exploration, and the willingness to love oneself well. We can become so busy with well-meaning agendas that we seldom devote time to learning who we are intrinsically, and create the things that would fill our hearts with glee. Connecting with our essence, discovering dormant dreams, and awakening extraordinary abilities is possible. Getting better acquainted with ourselves frees us to experiment with our potential and aspirations confidently. Let's take the time to learn who we are and what we're capable of. We can get better at harnessing our indomitable faculties and cultivating unfocused assets and abilities buried beneath our busy, distracted lives.

Music: Music, considered the universal language, stirs the soul. Our soul, the reservoir of our thoughts, beliefs, attitudes, moods, and emotions, can inspire and be inspired by beauty, love, and other virtues or resonate with dark, less harmonious energy. Music is also a mood maker; it can soothe, excite, and amplify our experience. It can shift our behavior and connect us with a spectrum of energetic frequencies. Consider that superheroes are not very heroic without epic-sounding music; scary movies aren't so frightening without eerie music; and love stories aren't so romantic without melancholy violins playing. Watch a movie and mute the music to a scene that's building in tension - it loses nearly all its intensity. It's a reverse but effective way to demonstrate music's power and influence on our mental and emotional states. Music creates an atmosphere. Select music for enjoyment, strategically set an environment, and charge the atmosphere with the energy you want to invoke.

Singing: Closely related to listening to music, singing is a melodic and artful expression of the soul. You don't have to be a professional singer or sing well to launch into an impromptu melody. Powerful lyrics encourage and reinforce our beliefs, affirm our convictions, and strengthen confidence and resolve. Vocalizing the words to a favorite song connects the singer with positive and compelling messages and moves emotionally. In sports, athletes may play a "theme song" to help them tap into the energy of the inner, conquering champion. Evoking a sense of love for the country, for example, many countries sing their national anthem at the opening of significant events.

Certain songs and soundtracks of movies remain popular for decades beyond their release. They conjure up feelings and memories of a significant time in the past. Likewise, singing songs that resonate and express joy, strength, and other virtues from your soul is self-honoring and affirming. It's a way to deepen self-appreciation and a sense of deserving and express the higher qualities of your being. So, sing and make a melody from your heart.

Meditation: This practice is about emptying the mind to rejuvenate and increase mental clarity. As you would erase a whiteboard or empty a trash receptacle, meditation clears the conscious mind of the excruciatingly large amount of information we take in during our waking hours. Much of the information we consume may not be very useful, but spending countless hours listening to and watching it is easy. If we were to add up all the time we spend on trivia each day and week, we would discover that it amounts to significant chunks of time over a lifespan.

Meditation is a way of releasing accumulated thoughts and information. A clean mental canvas and emptied receptacle help keep the mind focused, organized, and open to new ideas and perspectives. In the same way that mechanical machines need maintenance and downtime, this practice slows and provides rest from constant mental activity, declutters the mind, and prevents overwhelm, helping you navigate your day with increased clarity and finesse. Meditation provides a vital counterbalance to sensory overload, allowing us to step away from the constant input of data, find stillness, and refresh our mental gears.

Mindfulness: Akin to meditation, mindfulness intentionally chooses an object or idea and places it on the whiteboard of the mind and at the forefront of your attention. It directs the focus of your thoughts to the specific chosen object or subject of interest for a brief period. This practice builds concentration powers, strengthens the ability to focus, and prevents the mind from wandering and getting lost in the sea of distractions. Dedicating time to mindfulness strengthens your capacity to stay engaged with your vision and enhance your imaginative and creative abilities. I reference an excellent book on the topic for further reading.

Laughter: Healthy laughter is medicine, dispersing negative energy and relieving unhealthy stress. Laughter helps us manage our emotions and attitudes by releasing endorphins, which contribute to feelings of happiness. Finding or creating moments that bring laughter can transport an individual to a state of joy and ease, where all worries, concerns, and negative emotions dissipate. In these moments, one can experience a sense of carefree bliss that is unparalleled. The impacts of our environment and interrelationships are inescapable. We can love our family, enjoy spending time with others, and enjoy our jobs, coworkers, and associations. Nevertheless, relationships are sometimes frustrating and stress-inducing.

In the right circumstances, laughter can act as a cleansing agent that can quickly change the feeling tone of an otherwise unpleasant or stressful encounter and support emotional and mental well-being. Use healthy laughter to manage interactions that would otherwise ruin your good disposition. Although, on occasion, confronting inappropriate behavior may be necessary. We can take things more lightly and find humor without appearing insensitive or rude and dismiss negativity before it gains hold.

Dance: Another form of artistic expression - melodies and rhythms connect you to a frequency of fun that lifts you beyond the cares of mundane living and offers both physical and creative release. When hearing an upbeat song, your body innately responds to the rhythm with foot tapping or head swaying as if connected to an invisible puppet master. Depending on the setting, your entire body may fully engage in this liberty of motion, carried away by the beats, syncopations, and harmonies. Dancing invites lightheartedness as you vibe with this mode of inner connectedness. Freeing your body to move in rhythmic ways helps dissolve self-consciousness and anxiety and inspires creative flow. Not only does it allow the soul to experience joy and fun, but it's an escape from life's weighty issues and also offers beneficial exercise. Dance more, worry less.

Fellowship: I have not experienced anything more enriching in terms of group gatherings than being in the midst of like-minded, energetically in sync, and collaborative people. The environment is positively charged and palpable with goodwill when people have the same general interests and motivations. Discover gatherings where individuals see others as equally important and valued as themselves. We're all connected in our humanity and presence on the planet. If we choose, we can be complimentary to others, rather than competitive with them. Offer your unique gifts and talents to those who receive them and genuinely desire the best for all. Connect with people with whom you share mutual world views and who appreciate, cheer, and support one another. It's good to find your 'tribe.' Though it's not a substitute for self-discovery and personal development, connecting with the right people is enriching, exhilarating, and empowering.

Reading: Include reading and studying literature that increases your soul, not only your bank account. If you don't know where to begin to accomplish that, those listed at the back of this book may be a good starting point. The man or woman who will grow beyond their present circumstances invests time and resources in their personal growth. They love to learn and want to evolve, so they read and listen to books, take courses, and seek opportunities to receive training. Materials that impart wisdom open mental doors of awareness, and the one who engages with them can enjoy greater personal fulfillment and prosperity. Practical knowledge is essential, but it changes. Wisdom is enduring. As we learn and apply better understanding in our experiences, we become better individuals, strengthen our families, and contribute to the health and well-being of our communities in our time and for future generations.

Silence and Stillness: We operate in many roles in our lifetime, and the demand upon our intellect, experience, emotions, and bodies is depleting. Our identity and the life we've been granted is singular - we don't get another. But we often overlook the care we need for ourselves. The roles in which we perform duties and obligations are only partial expressions of our being. Careers or jobs are what we do for a time, but we're far more than the roles we fulfill. Intervals of quietness and stillness can refresh and reset mental and emotional energy and restore balance. Setting aside time to withdraw from the noise and demands of our roles helps us recharge. Allowing quietness in our environment helps us to decompress and be with ourselves without outside demands or distractions.

Reclining or sitting, add or eliminate objects or sounds that facilitate entering physical comfort and mental silence and stillness to enhance the experience. Closing the eyes helps tune out visual distractions and allows the mind to focus on simply being. If you're inclined, you can direct your attention to the various aspects of your physical being - your body, breathing, and hearing, for example. Notice the subtleties of the environment around you but, simultaneously, realize they are outside of you. You are not your body with its sensory faculties, but the observer. Recognize and appreciate the awareness of your being - your self-consciousness. Practicing stillness and silence helps to connect with the inner self and reduce stress.

Exercise: Light to moderate exercise relieves tension and contributes to the body's endurance, stamina, strength, conditioning, health, and overall well-being. A healthy, fit body is necessary to live fully and give the greatest energy to your vision. What good is a car engine without a working chassis and a functional body to transport the passenger or driver? And how long and far can one drive something that is broken down and unreliable? Regular exercise helps keep our bodies in good working order so that we can go where we want, do what we like, and more thoroughly enjoy our lives. Our life force is vibrant and active and seeks fuller expression through us. And it has provided a physical vessel through which we interface with and experience the world. Our responsibility is to care for and maintain our body while it's in our possession.

Fasting: Done with purpose, intentional intervals of abstinence from food and beverages have physical and spiritual benefits. Fasting helps rest bodily systems and redirects energy needed for maintenance and repair rather than processing food. Fasting also curbs the sensory desires that sometimes insist on unhealthy indulgences, helping to discipline unbridled appetites. Because the natural senses are subdued, the higher senses sharpen.

Intentional food abstinence can be challenging when eating is done to satisfy habit and not hunger. Abstaining from food and beverages other than water doesn't feel good at first, but it builds self-control and bodily discipline. Periodic or intervals of limiting food intake and other sensory stimuli also improve mental clarity and focus. Commend and appreciate yourself for any intervals of abstinence you complete. This way, fasting becomes a welcome activity rather than a dreaded requisite. Fasting can be a healthy habit - consult a medical professional for guidance and advice.

Nature: The visible universe and natural world hold awe-inspiring beauty and wonder. Deep, expansive oceans, majestic mountains, green plains, vast deserts, tree-filled forests, rolling hills, insects, birds, and other animals: our blue planet, immense stars, and innumerable galaxies all give us a glimpse into the remarkable invisible intelligence, power, and grandeur they represent. Scientific discoveries provide us with insight and understanding of our natural environment. We develop products and systems that allow us to gain great advantages from our natural environment.

When we look for it, the natural world can also teach us important and valuable lessons about how to effectively navigate life. I learned, for example, from a flower pressing through a crack in cement that persevered through seemingly impossible conditions to reach the light and fulfill its potential. From a lone, obscure blossom that radiated its vibrant colors and delicate petals despite being surrounded by a menagerie of untamed grass and leaves. And from the retreat into silent observance of forest animals as a higher order of beings quietly sauntered into their domain.

Pausing to appreciate the grand scale, unfathomable power, as well as intricate minute details of creation reminds us that we are part of something significant and magnificent, far greater than ourselves. Its immensity and complexity are impossible to comprehend fully, and it's empowering to consider that we are integral to this synchronous tapestry of life. Daily, we get the privilege of responding with delight, awe, and amazement. Creation's beauty, order, and design serve as a source of inspiration and a reminder of the power and artistry revealed in it. Practice inviting to your awareness that the intelligence, ability, power, and substance that brought the universe into being also brought you here at this time. Be inspired to bring forth and give your unique abilities, gifts, and talents.

Writing/Journaling: Although invisible, thoughts are things. Journaling expresses your thoughts and brings them into visible, tangible representation. Clothing your thoughts in written words helps to clarify, organize, and refine them and gives them definition and specificity. Your written vision is your dream inked in color and symbols, its first physical form. Writing it brings it into the material dimension and provides a visual road map for its achievement, using it as a referencing tool to remain focused and establish goals and action plans. Reading it acts as a stimulant, stirring your passion and fueling your intention, compelling you to act. Brainstorming with pen and paper can be like priming a pump when you want to generate new, fresh, and innovative ideas for effectively and efficiently advancing or expanding your vision. Allow the free flow of ideas without filtering or editing. Write them down as they come to you, and edit them after you've created a list. It's good practice for entering creative flow and an effective way to harvest solutions and new approaches.

Affirmations: Affirmations help us shape our reality by aligning our spoken words with the conditions we want. Because we speak from what we believe, pause and inspect your words before they leave your lips and impact your life or another's. Remember that we are connected, and our words and actions have a ripple effect beyond the present moment and our lives. Express the conditions you would love rather than those that appear. Speak in the affirmative. Believe that things will happen in your favor, and restrain the inclination to express in words to the contrary.

Practice affirming self-talk. Speaking well of yourself boosts self-esteem and improves relationships and overall outlook on life. You would not long enjoy the company of one who constantly complained and declared doubt, doom, gloom, disaster, or destruction. Speaking appreciatively and affirmingly of yourself generates positivity, releasing endorphins or 'feel good' hormones. Positive self-talk leads to positive actions and successful outcomes, forming a circuit that generates more affirming and optimistic speech and positive actions. Discipline yourself to reflect on the nature of your thoughts before speaking them aloud. You'll become more aware of your energetic presence, how thoughtless utterances create tone and atmosphere, and their effect on yourself and others.

Retreat/Pilgrimage: Getting away from the busyness of day-to-day demands and responsibilities can be a challenge. Family, work, and other obligations keep most people tethered to their environment. Planning to get away from demands and distractions can be stressful in itself. Aside from the entertainment and relaxation value of vacations or holidays, which are healthy and vital, retreats and pilgrimages are opportunities to dive deeper into a contemplative study or introspection. Taking time to learn, grow, and sharpen has many benefits, including deepening knowledge or skills training, enhanced work/life alignment, improved clarity, and increased efficiency. Sometimes, a retreat can mean unplugging electronics, turning off the phone and television, and uninstalling apps. Absconding from the nonessential creates space and time for connecting to the higher virtues of the soul. Such experiences enrich one's own life and enable them to offer more to others. Retreats can be at a physical locale or an online experience without leaving your home. The idea is that it is in an environment free from distraction and outside influences over a few days or longer. It's conducive to a deeper level of connection with self or others and provides opportunities and resources for studying, learning, or other immersive experiences.

Regular activities that engage the higher faculties and virtues are essential and anchor, strengthen, and increase mind, body, and spiritual expression. Their practice develops the inner infrastructure from which a deliberate, gratifying, and bountiful life is created.

17

Delivering Results

— ◆ —

"Ideas are easy. It's the execution of ideas that separate the sheep from the goats."

Sue Grafton

We all have generated results that reflect our repetitive, prevailing thoughts up until now. And we will continue to produce results if we're conscious and remain in our physical body. Unless we adopt new thinking habits, develop emotional discipline, and act differently than we have, over the following days, months, and years of our lives, we'll generate the same results with slight variation in details. Albert Einstein's definition of insanity – doing the same things and expecting a different result, sounds dismissively trite, but its insight is profound.

Creating a life that you love is about moving your vision forward until you have it in your experience. We will either be the participants and recipients of an advancing and prosperous world or the victims and collateral damage of a declining one. Both are equally possible and available. The desired life and experiences are within each one's power, and we're more than able to deliver new and more delightful results from an abundant and benevolent resident source. It cannot come by wishing or wanting. The things you love won't come about through comparing with others or being overly impressed with what they have. It won't come about by lamenting the lack of something in one's own experience or resenting others for what they have. And it certainly will not be gained by spending valuable energy and multiplied hours entertaining or placating with streaming services, social media, cable television, or other distracting activities.

Although relaxation and entertainment are essential to a balanced life, it's of supreme importance to discover and embrace your life's unique inner call. Invest valuable time learning new things that expand your awareness and develop healthy, constructive interests that help you express who you want to be and increase your enjoyment. We all have abilities we'd love to refine, qualities we'd love to enhance, traits we'd love to evolve, and habits we want to transform. And we can if we're willing. Living a life you love means thoughtless comments and parroting notions that contradict your vision can no longer be your default. It means you can no longer allow your un-evolved attitude, reactions, and mood to operate on autopilot. It means your belief about yourself and the world must be coherent, and the interest in your own good must equal the good you want for others. It means thinking and, subsequently, feeling differently.

Are there unwanted and unwelcome things that occur? Undoubtedly. But the good outweighs them overwhelmingly.

Continually give your energy and emotions to the lovely, noble, beautiful, commendable, virtuous, honest, and just. Filling your life with these virtues increases them in the world and is the light that overcomes darkness. Glance at the unwanted and unwelcome as you would something passing your peripheral sight. Release the pain of the past. Forgive the perceived shortcomings of others, and create a new narrative for who you choose to be and how you view others and interact with the world.

Delivering the life you imagine and deserve doesn't happen to or for you; it happens with you. It happens by deliberate design and intentional action. You are the architect and engineer of how you experience life. Why not design and build the life you love rather than allow fate to deliver months and years of frustration, angst, and disappointment? You are the highest form of life on the planet and deserve to have experiences that reflect that supreme status.

The results you want and welcome begin with new ideas but culminate in consistent action steps toward them. Having a dream but doing nothing towards obtaining it is only musing. Dream building is not just creating a vision for what you'd love - it's doing the interior self-work and practical exterior work daily, moving yourself and your dream ever closer to its materialization.

King Solomon said that dreams come by abundant effort. Another ancient luminary challenged his readers to prove their faith, void of action, while he demonstrated his faith by his corresponding actions.

Authentic faith claims have accompanying and complementary actions. Consistent, aligned action is the evidence that one believes.

To use a sports analogy, someone may have faith to hit a home run, but if they don't get up to the plate and swing the bat - they'll never get to first base, let alone hit a home run. Another may have faith to make a free throw in basketball, but if they never hoist the ball, they'll never make the basket or win the game. What abilities are you holding back? On what opportunities are you taking a pass? The abundance and prosperity of the universe are for you, too.

Beginning with what you authentically desire is paramount because it goes beyond having a goal. Acting in authentic purpose keeps you interested, engaged, enthusiastic, and determined. To fulfill your personal purpose and experience the life you love, your dream must come from within and resonate with what you want to express and how you want to show up in the world. There are many things one can do in one's lifetime. But when we lay our heads on our pillow for the last time, we all want to feel like we redeemed our time well, knowing that our life has been one of love and that we lived purposefully and without reservation.

Aligned actions are necessary because they keep you on task and prevent you from losing focus, becoming irretrievably distracted, and wasting your days and energy. Whatever holds your attention controls your life; what you stop giving attention to withers and fades. Once you have unearthed your inspiration and purpose - the thing you most want to be, do, have, share, and experience in the world, SET ABOUT

IT! Be unrelenting in giving expression to the creative force inspiring and compelling you. Consider what action, even small steps, you can take that aligns with what you have decided you want and KEEP TAKING ACTION! "It's always the doing that gets it done," my brother, Michael, often quips. It's a gentle and pointed reminder that genuine faith requires corresponding and consummating action.

There is something you can do EVERY DAY to realize your dreams and desires. Believe that you have every resource you need to take action toward your goal. Your actions don't need to be massive or costly. You don't need to know how your dream will manifest. Your role is to believe in, nurture, and distill it into smaller, doable, mostly enjoyable tasks every day while being efficient and effective.

Do what you can using what you have, and don't concern yourself with acting beyond your capacity. More will appear with each successive step; you always have more at your disposal than you can see. Sometimes, an action may be intangible, like visualizing, reviewing your written vision statement, or fueling and nurturing it with emotion, or brainstorming ideas. Give yourself the gift of patience and forgiveness while building your dream. No one achieves their dream by a flawless process. Don't linger over missteps; accept them as feedback for your journey and improve and advance with the next step.

Live presently! Forget the hurts and pain of the past because keeping it alive in your thoughts and emotions keeps it happening in your present experience. Remember the good! There's good in every situation, circumstance, and condition you encounter, whether within your awareness or not. Sometimes, you'll have to look more intently and longer to find it, but good is always present. Insisting upon this will prevent you from being mired in disappointment, despondence, and other contractive mental and emotional states that do not serve your life.

Be determined to focus on the desire, not the obstacles that appear as you move forward. Mountains do move if you persist. Stay emotionally engaged with the feelings of already possessing what you have designed and decreed because you do -in the form of your mental vision. Hold the vision in your heart and mind with the same confidence as you will when it's in your actual experience. And because all things are possible with divine assistance, you will deliver it into your tangible reality.

Remember that delivering results you love is more than taking action every day, large or small, towards your dream - it begins with transforming who you have been up until now. Inwardly, you must be a different person than who you have been up until now. To build a life you truly love, establish a strong foundation of self-awareness, personal responsibility, self-reliance, and self-empowerment. These pillars are not just important; they are essential to achieving your dreams and living at higher levels of fulfillment. Renew your mind and unleash its full potential. Dare to challenge your existing paradigms and tap into your divine faculties of imagination, intuition, perception, and memory. Take authority over your thoughts, seize control of the direction of your life, and break free from self-imposed limitations.

Living a life you truly love is the ultimate compliment you can give yourself, the greatest example to set for those around you, the highest way to honor the precious gift of life you have been given and the greatest service you can offer the world. Others are waiting for your creative flow that brings beauty, joy, wonder, hope, and inspiration to the lives you will touch. The impact of your gift will reverberate when you offer it and be received with great gratitude and appreciation. It's a meaningful and appropriate response to the creative intelligence and power that sustains you. You are a glorious, powerful stream of creative genius.

18

Dimensional Thinking

—◇—

"A mind that is stretched by a new experience can never go back to its old dimensions"

Holmes.

Currency, as traditionally defined, is a system of money used to facilitate the exchange of goods and services. But another currency is superior and exchanges in a different domain than monetary currency. It's the currency of our thoughts and feelings, which we exchange for the experiences we have. You are beginning to appreciate and acquire this spiritual currency and to understand that living the inspired life that beckons you is your right, privilege, and responsibility. Only your time, attention, and commitment are necessary to deliver it into your experience. The reservoir of persistent thoughts and feelings is the scaffold and foundation upon which life experiences are constructed, and experiencing it in the way we love is within our power and authority.

Your vision is real and exists in a form seen only by the imagination, the eye of the mind. New doors of awareness and pathways to fulfillment and prosperity are appearing and opening to you. Like the law of gravity and electricity, the immutable law of prosperity and the unlimited source of wealth is available to everyone who will enjoin it according to the methods and means established. The substance of your dream is the imaginal and emotional blueprint that you hold. Its path to manifestation is your unyielding faith that it is yours and your purpose to have it. And how it will come to you is through your aligned, consistent, and efficient actions. The Intelligent Universe will serve and supply you with all that's required in ways you cannot entirely know or appreciate. Your role is to dream the highest, most authentic life you can imagine for yourself (for all things are possible), believe in yourself and it, and do the things that bring it to you. The Intelligent Universe's role is to transmute your vision into tangible and material reality for you and those whom you influence and impact.

The chair you sit in, the car you drive, the clothes you wear, and the Internet with which you access this book all began as a thought and originate in a reality that cannot be seen with the natural eye. Everything begins in the invisible before we experience it. Having a life filled with the results we love requires that we become the curator of our thinking. Our thoughts and feelings, and how we manage them, determine what life looks and feels like in the days and years to come. Feelings, whether of love, joy, courage, wonder, amusement, pride of achievement, fear, anger, resentment, guilt, and shame, all have their basis in what we think and believe.

The Results Formula reminds us that the ideas that we are exposed to generate more thoughts to which we assign meaning and form opinions. Some become firmly held, highly charged beliefs. When our beliefs and associated emotions have germinated, like the shoots of seeds planted, they pierce into the fabric of our lives. They show up as either fragrant and fruitful plants in a carefully cultivated garden or as weeds and thorns choking the good and needing uprooting.

You never need to compromise your values, take unfair advantage or what belongs to others to get what you want. Do what you can, from where you are, with what you have, and more will be provided. You will be supplied with all that is necessary for the next step. Be anxious for nothing - you have the resources and support of the Intelligent Universe as your benefactor and partner.

Do not require the good opinions of others to validate your vision. No one can determine your unique purpose, define the desires of your heart, or estimate the worthiness of your gifts and talents. Fulfill your purpose and deliver your gifts; the people who need, want, and appreciate them will appear. Neither do you need to neglect areas of your life to advance another. Let your effort be balanced. Embrace a welcoming and grateful approach to the roles your life encompasses. It is all working together for your increase and betterment. Always remember your connection to Infinite Intelligence and divine activity. It maintains as its highest interest your good. These guiding principles will keep you encouraged, strengthened, balanced, and filled with hope.

Waking to the reality of your higher inner self is the ultimate empowerment. With this knowledge, you can begin to fearlessly chart and steer the course of your life. Happiness and success depend on the extent to which your higher faculties have predominance over the conditioned habits and reactions of the lower senses that keep you in the status quo. Without this subjugation of the lower senses to the higher, the patterns of thinking, feeling, and acting will continue to dominate and produce unwanted results.

Uninformed and unbridled lower senses that steer our lives are at the root of our discontent. To resolve problems and dissolve discontent, we must access, trust, rely on, and be guided by the part of our being with the answers and solutions. Superficial interests and things have their temporary appeal; however, seek first to satisfy the essential needs of your soul and express its virtues. This will put you in harmony with the universal good and your unique purpose. What you are in harmony with, you gravitate toward and attract.

Improved results in your life start with improved ideas! Be willing to let go of the thinking and beliefs that have produced unwanted, unwelcome results. Prepare your mind each day, and don't allow random thoughts to flourish; take the reigns of your own thoughts. Begin with gratitude, empowering ideas, and positive attitudes, and maintain them throughout the day, no matter what you encounter. Don't beat yourself up if you get off track; just get back on. Adopt winning perspectives and establish healthy, optimistic ways to perceive your world, always looking for the good.

Presumably, everyone reading or listening to this book will receive another year of life. That's a lot of time currency to work with, and we could all make significant progress and improvements with it. What value will you exchange for your year of time currency? What would you love to transform in the next twelve months? What changes in your life would you welcome?

Staying in personal growth and development content is the transformational oil of an advancing life. Automobiles, if they are to function as intended, not only need fuel, but their engines require a supply of lubricating oil to function efficiently, effectively, and continually. Without them, the engine fails, locks up, and forward motion halts. To supply your new life with fuel and oil to keep growing, advancing, and thriving, keep reading and listening to ROADDmap and materials like it.

Throughout this book, we've uncovered four exceptional faculties with which we are endowed, and consciously employing them can give rise to our dreams. Exploring the depths of these superior attributes and their immense creative potential is beyond the scope of this writing. A rudimentary understanding, however, is integral to tapping personal potential, and I'll briefly review them here:

Imagination: Imagination is your inventive and visioning faculty. Imagination allows you to create the stories, images, events, and things that represent the life you would love with the simple yet powerful act of deliberate thought. You can enjoy rich and deeply meaningful experiences and do magnificent things imaginally. In fact, it must be your persistent thought before it becomes your actual experience. Remember, thoughts are the architects of destiny - nothing comes to be without first existing as thought. Harness the boundless potential of your imagination and vividly conjure images of what you love. What is the highest, authentic vision you can create for yourself? The same intelligent power with which you can conceive it will work with and for you to realize it.

Perception: Perception is another ocular faculty that allows us to frame how we view ourselves and the world. Use this mental faculty to see yourself living the life you love. Holding a positive and loving self-image is vital because you cannot elevate your circumstances beyond how you truly see yourself. Believe in your innate ability to achieve your desires and express, in attitude and actions, the person experiencing your dream. Be the person taking the actions. That is how dreams are brought from the invisible and immaterial state into reality.

The faculty of perception also allows us to see the good around us and in our circumstances. Though not always apparent to the natural senses, advantages can come from every difficulty or challenge. Retrain your mind to keep an optimistic, charitable, and gracious point of view. Don't entertain the seeming baser actions of people; they will have their due recompense. See the world's condition as improving, seek to improve yourself, and make your contribution to an advancing world.

We are indeed privileged to live in a world with abundant opportunities. Feel empowered to exceed the limits others have set for you and pursue your highest dreams because universal intelligence, abundance, and power are at your disposal. Use the faculty of perception to overwrite negative thinking that has limited your life. Undo paradigms by redefining beliefs that have been held with negative energy. By assigning new meanings and understandings to them, you will unshackle yourself from the painful past, serve the good you want to enjoy presently, and allow yourself to embrace a more exciting and delightful future.

Intuition: The Infinite, by definition, encompasses everything, past, present, and future. Intuition is your connection to its unlimited knowledge and wisdom. It provides guidance, counsel, and answers about matters unknowable by the five natural senses. Sometimes, without prompting, guidance, instruction, or information may inexplicably come into your awareness. You may have experienced a nudge from your intuition with a sudden inclination to grab an umbrella, though the sky is sunny and humidity low, only to later be caught in a sudden downpour. Perhaps a sudden uneasiness about a decision you were about to make helped you change direction and avoid a problem.

Developing sensitivity to your inner voice of intuition is possible by engaging with it proactively and regularly. There is nothing unknown by Infinite Intelligence, including thoughts, motivations, and plans. Although we often don't hear or heed it, intuition is always reliable and trustworthy. By harnessing the power of intuition, we can avail ourselves of assistance and benefits and avoid needless difficulties and setbacks. Listen to the whispers of your intuition. Embrace it and unlock the advantages it brings.

Memory: Memory is our recall faculty. It calls up for us the significant and impactful impressions contained in the mind. Our minds can retrieve imagery and sensory experiences from the projected future just as easily as the past. Using memory to recall the details and dynamics of the vision held can be used to a great benefit. Recalling or visualizing an anticipated future state deepens its impression in the subconscious mind. This is important because our lives are defined by the contents of our subconscious, where life-governing habits are formed. Adding emotions to our visualization energetically charges it causing the elements of our vision to come together and manifest in reality.

These faculties are under your control, and your greater potential is unlocked by developing skills in harnessing them. Although we are conditioned to be influenced by external factors, with practice and learning, we can take control of our lives and create a purposeful and fulfilling journey. Otherwise, we wander through life as though in the wilderness, having sufficient food and shelter but missing out on bounteous and benevolent promises. You are worthy and deserving of achieving your dreams, and have everything you need to create it. It can be challenging to change the patterns that have shaped your life so far, but you are capable of doing it. Transformation isn't hard, but it requires introspection, self-reflection, expanded awareness, desire, courage, patience, and fortitude. You can rely on your inherent superior qualities and remarkable capacities to deliver the results to which you assign and engage them.

Since you're engaging in this content, you've already taken the first steps. Once you understand the personal authority and liberty that comes from using the principles of ROADDmap, you won't want to go back to your old ways and remain there. You'll love discovering the depths of your potential and creative ability. It's your life, and you deserve to live it in a way that brings you increasing joy. Follow your passions, pursue your dreams, and don't settle for anything less than a life that makes your heart sing. It's within your capability, and it's your option to do so or not. The choice is yours alone. If you will live the life you love, discover your purpose - the thing for which you are here, and express it. Proactively engage your higher faculties, mind, and emotions in the way herein described.

Every day, you choose how you will respond, what you will say, what you will do, what you will entertain, what you will believe, and how you will feel. You are the empowered authority of your experience. You may not have chosen your human form, but you do choose how you engage with life and express your being. If you want something different or a higher quality of life experience, ROADDmap's transformational principles can help you achieve it.

My hope is that you feel inspired and compelled to discover your purpose, pursue your authentic desires, and live the life you love. Read or listen to this book or portions of it often to engage with its transformative content and relentlessly practice the principles and skills you learn. By doing so, you will overwrite the subconscious patterns that have shackled your potential and imprint new ones that empower, enrich, and elevate your life.

Think dimensionally. There is something wonderful in you that longs to come forth. Listen to its signals and answer its call. Stay curious about what's possible - living an adventuresome, extraordinary life is within your reach. You're far more than you think you are and than you have experienced so far. The universe is for you and the life energy that sustains you is intelligent, powerful, infinite, and desires to express itself through you, for you, and as you in the world.

You're moving beyond self-doubt, self-sabotage, and procrastination. You're increasing in mental currency and unmovable confidence in yourself, your dreams, and your ability to achieve them. You're beginning to live the life you absolutely love.

For Further Reading

—◆—

Embarking on a path to self-improvement and building a fulfilling life is a personal journey. It involves getting in touch with your innermost self, identifying your sources of inspiration, and utilizing your inherent cognitive abilities to create he experiences that bring you joy. You can either choose to embrace this opportunity or let it pass you by. If you decide to take this journey, the following books can serve as valuable resources to help you along the way.

"As a Man Thinketh" by James Allen is a timeless self-help classic that explores the profound impact of our thoughts on our lives. This concise and powerful book argues that our thoughts are the seeds of our destiny, shaping our character and influencing our actions. He emphasizes the importance of cultivating positive, constructive thoughts to create a life of purpose, success, and fulfillment.

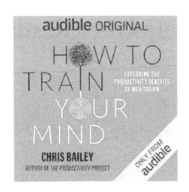

"How to Train Your Mind" by Chris Bailey digs deep into the practical, tactical benefits of integrating a meditation ritual into your life. In addition to calming your mind and allowing you to slow down in an overanxious world, Chris Bailey shows that meditation can de-stimulate your mind so you can think more clearly, procrastinate less, and be more effective at everything you do - at work and at home.

"The Magic Power of Self-Image Psychology" by Maxwell Maltz delves into the profound influence of self-image on a person's success and overall well-being. Maltz explores how individuals can transform their lives by reshaping their self-image and beliefs, ultimately achieving their goals and realizing their potential. Through practical techniques and insights, the book offers a roadmap for harnessing the magic of self-image psychology to attain personal growth and success.

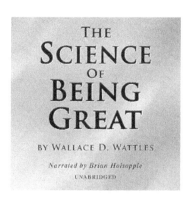

"The Science of Being Great" by Wallace D. Wattles is a timeless self-help book that explores the principles of personal growth and greatness. Wattles argues that anyone can achieve greatness by aligning their thoughts and actions with universal laws, emphasizing the importance of self-belief, purposeful effort, and a deep understanding of one's own potential.

"You Squared" by Price Pritchett is a concise and powerful book that challenges conventional thinking and encourages readers to break through their limitations and achieve extraordinary results. Through a brief and impactful narrative, Pritchett introduces the concept of exponential thinking, guiding readers to overcome self-imposed boundaries and unlock their true potential by embracing a new perspective on life and success.

ABOUT THE AUTHOR

Heddy Toure is a mother and grandmother to four amazing grandchildren. She is an author, DreamBuilder® Coach, inspirational speaker, and workshop leader who is passionate about helping people discover their dreams and turn them into reality. She uses her proprietary ROADDmap framework:

Recognizing Who You Are and What You Want

Overwriting Limiting Patterns and Habits

Accessing and Harnessing Your Hidden Gift

Delivering Your Dreams by Doing the Work

Dimensional Thinking Through Challenges

to help others unearth their dreams and unique purpose, reveal their innate ability, restore personal authority, and harness their indomitable power to live the life they can imagine. Heddy continues to study and train with world-class teachers and coaches to develop and improve her unique ability to help people connect with their inner voice, and discover their great worth and undeniable potential.

For more information, email
TalktoHeddy@gmail.com or visit **www.TalktoHeddy.com**.

Made in the USA
Middletown, DE
18 May 2024

54372228R00089